The Lutheran Handbook

About "Winking Luther"

Martin Luther's theology is grounded in paradoxes—sinner/saint, law/gospel, hidden/revealed—and illuminated by a down-to-earth, everyday sense of humor. This icon of Luther winking at the reader combines the serious, formal scholarship that was his life's work with the humor and lightheartedness that characterized his personality.

The wink on Luther's face indicates that even though theology is serious stuff, we should nonetheless remember that it is not our theology that saves us, but Jesus Christ. Therefore, our life in the church can be buoyant, and our theological wranglings can be done with a sense of humor and love for our neighbor.

The Lutheran Handbook

Augsburg Fortress
Minneapolis

Content editor: Kristofer Skrade
Cover design: Diana Running
Production editors: Ivy Palmer and James Satter
Interior illustrations: Brenda Brown

Contributing writers: Suzanne Burke, Lou Carlozo, Giacomo Cassese, Mark Gardner, Wes Halula, Sarah Henrich, Mark Hinton, Sue Houglum, Rolf Jacobson, Susan M. Lang, Andrea Lee, Daniel Levitin, Terry Marks, Catherine Malotky, Jeffrey S. Nelson, Rebecca Ninke, Eliseo Pérez-Álvarez, Dawn Rundman, Jonathan Rundman, Ted Schroeder, Ken Sundet Jones, Hans Wiersma

ISBN 0-8066-5179-2

CONTENTS

Everyday Stuff   85

Bible Stuff

Luther's Small Catechism

This Book Belongs To

Name _____

Address _____

_____

E-mail _____

Telephone _____

Birth date _____

Baptismal birth date _____

First communion _____

Confirmation date _____

Godparents' (baptismal sponsors') names

_____

_____

_____

_____

Churches I've belonged to:	*Years of membership*
_____	_____
_____	_____
_____	_____
_____	_____
_____	_____
_____	_____

✠

About My Congregation

Name _____

Address _____

_____

Year organized/founded _____

My pastor(s) _____

_____

_____

_____

Number of baptized members _____

Average weekly worship attendance _____

Facts about my denomination _____

_____

_____

_____

Other information about my congregation and faith

_____

_____

_____

_____

✠

PREFACE

Please Be Advised:

Lots of books, pamphlets, and booklets have been written through the centuries as companions for average folks who wanted help navigating their way through a complicated subject. *The Boy Scout Handbook* comes to mind, for example. So do *The American Red Cross First Aid and Safety Handbook*, *Tune and Repair Your Own Piano: A Practical and Theoretical Guide to the Tuning of All Keyboard Stringed Instruments*, and *National Audubon Society's Field Guide to North American Reptiles and Amphibians*. They stand as testimony to the average person's need for a guide to both the vast truths and complex detail that make up a particular area of interest. These books turn complicated, inaccessible ideas into simple, easy-to-understand concepts, and, if necessary, into action steps that are easy to follow.

Likewise, *The Lutheran Handbook* follows this format. Here, you will discover a combination of reliable, historical, and theological information alongside some fun facts and very practical tips on being a churchgoing follower of Jesus Christ, all presented in that oh-so-Lutheran, down-to-earth, tongue-in-cheek sort of way.

You will also discover that this book is intended for learning and enjoyment. (Some Lutherans have trouble doing the latter until they've first suffered through the former.) It's meant to spur conversation, to inform and edify, and to make you laugh. Think of the book as a comedian with a dry sense of humor and a degree in theology. It can be used in the classroom with students or at the dinner table with family or in solitude.

But however you use it, use it! We've cut the corners off so you can throw it in your backpack or stuff it in a pocket. It's printed on paper that accepts either ink or pencil nicely, so feel free to write and highlight in it (and there's room for notes in the back). The cover is this fancy, nearly indestructible stuff that will last forever too, so don't worry about spilling soda pop or coffee on it. We've even heard it can sustain a direct hit from a nuclear missile.

Anyway, the point is this: Being a follower of Jesus is hard enough without having to navigate the faith journey—let alone the maze of church culture—all alone. Sooner or later everyone needs a companion.

—THE EDITORS

CHURCH STUFF

Every well-prepared Lutheran should have a basic understanding of Lutheran teachings and where they came from.

Plus, since every church goes about worship in a slightly different way, it might take a little time to get the hang of things—especially if you're new to a congregation.

This section includes:

- Essential facts about the Lutheran faith. (If you know these things, you'll know more than most.)

- Practical advice for singing hymns, taking communion, and getting to know the people in your congregation.

- Hints for enjoying worship—even when you're having a bad day.

HOW TO GET TO KNOW YOUR PASTOR

Pastors play an important role in the daily life of your congregation and the community. Despite their churchly profession, fancy robes, and knowledge of Greek, pastors experience the same kinds of ups and downs as everyone else. They value member efforts to meet, connect with, and support them.

❶ **Connect with your pastor after worship.**
After the worship service, join others in line to shake the pastor's hand. Sharing a comment about the sermon, readings, or hymns lets the pastor know that his or her worship planning time is appreciated. If your congregation doesn't practice the dismissal line, find other ways to make that personal connection.

❷ **Pray daily for your pastor, because he or she doesn't just work on Sunday.**
Your pastor has many responsibilities, like visiting members in the hospital, writing sermons, and figuring out who can help drain the flooded church basement. In your prayers, ask God to grant your pastor health, strength, and wisdom to face the many challenges of leading a congregation.

❸ **Ask your pastor to share with you why he or she entered ordained ministry.**
There are many reasons why a pastor may have enrolled in seminary to become an ordained minister. Be prepared for a story that may surprise you.

❹ Stop by your pastor's office to talk, or consider making an appointment to get to know him or her. Pastors welcome the opportunity to connect with church members at times other than worship. As you would with any drop-in visit, be sensitive to the fact that your pastor may be quite busy. A scheduled appointment just to chat could provide a welcome break in your pastor's day.

Getting to know your pastor can help you to get more out of church.

HOW TO SURVIVE FOR ONE HOUR IN AN UN-AIR-CONDITIONED CHURCH

Getting trapped in an overheated sanctuary is a common churchgoing experience. The key is to minimize your heat gain and electrolyte loss.

❶ Plan ahead.
When possible, scout out the sanctuary ahead of time to locate optimal seating near fans or open windows. Consider where the sun will be during the worship service and avoid sitting under direct sunlight. Bring a bottle of water for each person in your group.

❷ Maintain your distance from others.
Human beings disperse heat and moisture as a means of cooling themselves. An average-size person puts off about as much heat as a 75-watt lightbulb. The front row will likely be empty and available.

❸ Remain still.
Fidgeting will only make your heat index rise.

Use your bulletin as a personal fan to keep cool.

❹ Think cool thoughts.
Your mental state can affect your physical disposition. If the heat distracts you from worship, imagine you're sitting on a big block of ice.

❺ Dress for survival.
Wear only cool, breathable fabrics.

❻ Avoid acolyte or choir robes when possible.
Formal robes are especially uncomfortable in the heat. If you must wear one, make sure to wear lightweight clothes underneath.

❼ Pray.
Jesus survived on prayer in the desert for 40 days. Lifting and extending your arms in an open prayer position may help cool your body by dispersing excess heat. If you've been perspiring, though, avoid exposing others to your personal odor.

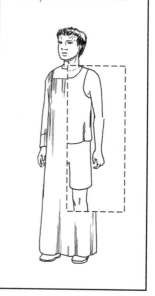

On hot days, wear light clothing underneath acolyte or choir robes.

Be Aware

- Carry a personal fan—or use your bulletin as a substitute.
- Worship services scheduled for one hour sometimes will run long. Plan ahead.

HOW TO RESPOND WHEN SOMEONE SITS IN YOUR PEW

We all carry a bubble of personal space. For some people, it's several feet. For others, it's about a millimeter. Wherever on the spectrum you happen to fall, there are certain situations in which we invite visitors into our little sphere of experience—like at church. Furthermore, human beings are territorial in nature and sometimes see strangers inside the bubble as an affront. These situations need not be cause for alarm.

❶ Smile and greet the "intruders."
Oftentimes they are visitors to your congregation—new blood. Avoid creating bad blood you might regret later on. Make solid eye contact so they know you mean it, shake hands with them, and leave no impression that they've done something wrong.

❷ View the "intrusion" as an opportunity.
Remember, you don't own the pew; you just borrow it once a week. Take the opportunity to get out of your rut and sit someplace new. This will physically emphasize a change in your perspective and may yield new spiritual discoveries.

❸ If you can tell that your new friends feel uncomfortable at having displaced you, despite your efforts to the contrary, make an extra effort to welcome them.
Consider taking them to brunch after church to become acquainted. If there are too many for you to foot the bill, consider inviting them to accompany you on a "go Dutch" basis. This will eliminate any hierarchy and place you on equal footing.

HOW TO USE A
WORSHIP BULLETIN

Many Lutheran congregations offer a printed resource called a bulletin to assist worshipers. The bulletin may contain the order of the service, liturgical information, music listings, the day's Bible readings, and important community announcements.

❶ Arrive early.
A few extra minutes before worship will allow you to scan the bulletin and prepare for the service.

❷ Receive the bulletin from the usher.
Upon entering the worship space, an usher will give you a bulletin. Some congregations stack bulletins near the entrance for self-service.

❸ Review the order of worship.
When seated, open the bulletin and find the order of the service, usually printed on the first or second page. Some churches print the entire service in the bulletin so worshipers don't have to switch back and forth between worship aids.

❹ Determine if other worship resources are required.
The order of worship may specify additional hymnals, song sheets, candles, or other external supplies required during the service.

❺ Fill out the attendance card.
A card may be located inside the bulletin or somewhere in your row. Fill it out completely. You may be asked to pass this card to an usher or to place it in the offering plate. Some congregations have visitors/communion attendance books for people to sign.

6 Reflect on bulletin artwork.

Covers often feature a drawing or design that corresponds to the season of the church year or the day's Bible verses. Examine the artwork and make a note of its connection to the lessons or sermon.

7 Track your worship progress.

The bulletin will guide you through the liturgy, hymns, and lessons as you worship and let you know where you are at all times.

8 Watch for liturgical dialogues.

The bulletin may contain spoken parts of the liturgy not found in the hymnal. The worship leader's parts may be marked with a "P:" or "L:". The congregation's responses may be marked with a "C:" and are often printed in boldface type.

9 Identify the worship leaders and assistants.

The names of ushers, musicians, greeters, readers, acolytes, and pastors usually can be found in the bulletin. Greet these people by name following the service. Make good eye contact.

10 Review the printed announcements.

Community activities, calendars, and updates are often listed in the back of the bulletin. Scan listings during the prelude music, the offering, or the spoken announcements.

11 Make good use of the bulletin after the service.

Some congregations re-use bulletins for later services. Return the bulletin if possible. Recycling bins may also be provided. If you wish, or unless otherwise instructed, you may take the bulletin home with you.

Be Aware

- Bulletins often use letter or color codes to signify which hymnals should be used. Look for a key or legend that details this information.

- Many church secretaries and worship committees need help preparing the bulletin each week. You may want to volunteer to copy, fold, or assemble the bulletin for an upcoming service.

- Most congregations stand at certain times during worship, such as to honor Jesus' presence when the Gospel is read. Standing and sitting—even occasional kneeling—aren't for exercise. Rather, they're an important physical participation in worship that helps you focus on the meaning behind the action.

If you choose not to save your worship bulletin, be sure to recycle it whenever possible.

HOW TO SING A HYMN

Music is an important part of the Lutheran tradition and an enjoyable way to build community. Hymn singing can be done without demonstrable emotion, but many otherwise stoic Lutherans appropriately channel emotion into their hymn singing and are therefore loud.

❶ Locate hymns in advance.
As you prepare for worship, consult the worship bulletin or the hymn board to find numbers for the day's hymns. Bookmark these pages in the hymnal using an offering envelope or attendance card.

❷ Familiarize yourself with the hymns.
Examine the composer credits, the years the composer(s) lived, and whether the tune has a different name than the hymn itself. Note how the hymn is categorized in the hymnal. Many hymnals group the songs into categories, such as "Society" and "Christmas."

❸ Assist nearby visitors or children.
Using a hymnal can be confusing. If your neighbor seems disoriented, help them find the correct pages, or let them read from your book.

❹ Adopt a posture for best vocal performance.
Hold the hymnal away from your body at chest level. Place one hand under the spine of the binding, leaving the other hand free to turn the pages. Keep your chin up so your voice projects outward.

5 Begin singing.
If the hymn is unfamiliar, sing the melody for the first verse. If you read music, explore the written harmony parts during the remaining verses. Loud-singing neighbors may or may not be in tune, so follow them with caution.

Support the hymnal's spine with one hand. Place the other on the open page.

6 Focus on the hymn's content.
Some of the lyrics may connect with a scripture reading of the day. Certain ones may be especially inspiring.

7 Avoid dreariness.
Hymns are often sung in such a serious way that the congregation forgets to enjoy the music. Sing with energy and feeling.

Be Aware

- Hymnals are not just for use at church. Consider keeping a personal copy of your congregation's hymnal at home for further reference and study. Hymnals also make excellent baptism or confirmation gifts.

- Some hymns use words and phrases that are difficult to understand (such as, "Here I raise my Ebenezer," from the hymn "Come Thou Fount of Every Blessing"). Use a dictionary or a Bible with a concordance to clear up any uncertainty.

HOW TO SING A PRAISE SONG

Many Lutheran congregations use modern worship styles, often called Praise & Worship (P&W), featuring guitars and drums. In these settings the words are typically displayed on large, multimedia projection screens.

❶ Follow the instructions of the song leader.
Someone in the praise band will invite the congregation to stand up, sit down, repeat certain sections, or divide into men's and women's vocal parts. Pay attention to this person to avoid getting off track.

❷ Learn the melody and song structure.
Pay special attention to the melody line sung by the band's lead vocalist. Praise & Worship songs can be tricky because they are rarely printed with notated sheet music and are sung differently from place to place.

❸ Sing along with gusto.
Once the melody has been introduced, join in the singing. When you're comfortable with the song, experiment with harmony parts.

❹ Avoid "zoning out."
Singing lyrics that are projected on giant screens can result in a glazed-over facial expression. Avoid this by surveying the worship area, noticing paraments and liturgical symbols, and making eye contact with other people.

❺ Identify lyrical themes.
Determine if the song is being used as a confession, a prayer, a hymn of praise, or serves another purpose.

❻ Watch out for raised hands.
Some Lutherans emote while singing contemporary
Christian songs and may suddenly raise their hands in
praise to God. Be sure to give these worshipers plenty
of room to avoid losing your eyeglasses.

Be Aware

- Lutheran worship is highly participatory. The praise
  band is there to help you and the congregation to sing
  and participate in worship, not to perform a concert.

- There are no strict prohibitions in the Lutheran
  tradition against physical expression during worship.

- In some congregations, praise gestures will draw amused
  stares.

*Beware of especially passionate worshipers
who might raise their hands too quickly.*

HOW TO LISTEN TO A SERMON

Lutherans believe God's Word comes to us through the sacraments and the preaching of Holy Scripture. Honoring God's Word, not to mention getting something out of church, includes diligent listening to the sermon and active mental participation.

❶ Review active listening skills.
While the listener in this case doesn't get to speak, the sermon is still a conversation. Make mental notes as you listen. Take notice of where and why you react and which emotions you experience.

❷ Take notes.
Note-taking promotes active listening and provides a good basis for later reflection. It also allows you to return to confusing or complicated parts at your own leisure. Some congregations provide space in the bulletin for notes, and many confirmation ministries provide structured worksheets.

Take notes to recall more information and get more out of the sermon.

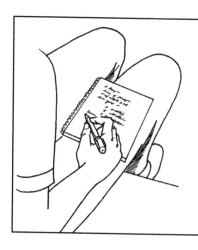

Try taking notes in an outline form so you can keep up without missing good information.

❸ **Maintain good posture. Avoid slouching.**
Sit upright with your feet planted firmly on the ground and your palms on your thighs. Beware of the impulse to slouch, cross your arms, or lean against your neighbor, as these can encourage drowsiness.

❹ **Listen for the law.**
You may feel an emotional pinch when the preacher names the sinner in you. Pay attention to your reaction, and try to focus on waiting for the gospel rather than becoming defensive. For more information, see "How to Tell the Difference Between the Law and the Gospel" on page 86.

❺ **Listen for the gospel.**
This will come in the form of a sentence most likely starting with the name Jesus and ending with the words *for you.* Upon hearing the gospel, you may feel a physical lightness, as though you've set down a great burden. You may cry tears of joy. This is normal.

❻ End by saying, "Amen."
Since preaching is mostly God's work, honor the Word by sealing the moment with this sacred word, which means, "It is most certainly true!"

❼ Review.
If you've taken written notes, read through them later that day or the next day and consider corresponding with the preacher if you have questions or need clarification. If you've taken mental notes, review them in a quiet moment. Consider sharing this review time with others in your congregation or household on a weekly basis.

HOW TO RESPOND TO A DISRUPTION DURING WORSHIP

Disruptions during worship are inevitable. The goal is to soften their impact.

❶ Simply ignore the offending event, if possible. Many disruptions are brief and the persons involved act quickly to quiet them. Avoid embarrassing others; maintain your attention on the worship activity.

❷ Some disruptions cannot be ignored and may threaten to continue indefinitely. The agony will go on unless you act. Consider the following types:

Active Children

- *Your Problem:* You are most familiar with your own family. If you sense an outburst will end quickly, simply allow it to pass. If not, escort the child to the lobby for a little quiet time, then return.

Try to ignore worship interruptions you think will end soon.

Note: Under all circumstances, children should be made to feel welcome in worship!

- *Someone Else's Problem:* Politely offer to help, perhaps by helping to occupy the child quietly or—with the parents' permission—by escorting the tot to the lobby, nursery, or cry room.

Personal Electronics

- *Your Problem:* Turn off cell phones, pagers, and other electronic alarms immediately and discreetly. If contact is made and it is critical, remove yourself to the lobby and call back. Under no circumstances should you answer your phone during worship.

Turn off all personal electronic devices before worship.

- *Someone Else's Problem:* Politely ask them to respect worship by moving the conversation to the lobby.

Chatty Neighbor

- *Your Problem:* Chatty persons should be alert to stares and grim looks from neighbors and be prepared to stop talking upon seeing them.

- *Someone Else's Problem:* Politely ask the talkers to wait until after worship to conclude the conversation. During the coffee hour, approach them with a cookie to mend any offense they may have felt.

Cameras

- *Your Problem:* Ask first if cameras are allowed. If so, unobtrusively and discreetly position yourself out of the line of sight of other worshipers. Be aware of the film's exposure number to avoid jarring auto-rewind noises. Flash cameras are *strictly* taboo.

- *Someone Else's Problem:* Politely offer to show the photographer where to stand to get the shot but without obstructing worship.

Sound System Feedback

- Pastors often make jokes to cover for feedback and keep the appropriate mood for worship. If this happens, consider making a donation earmarked for a "new sound system" in the plate.

Be Aware

- Some people may perceive tennis shoes with light-up soles on acolytes and other worship assistants to be disruptive. If possible, coordinate the color of the shoe lights with the season of the church year to avoid undue flak.

THE ANATOMY OF A BAPTISM

Pastors preside at baptisms to ensure good order.

Pouring water on the baptized person, the pastor says, "I baptize you in the name of the Father, and of the Son, and of the Holy Spirit."

God is the true actor in baptism, bringing everyone involved to the font and inspiring trust and faith.

Sponsors (godparents) are on hand to support those being baptized and to make baptismal promises on behalf of children. The whole congregation joins in these promises and pledges their support also.

Typically a baptismal candle is lit and presented to show that the newly-baptized person has received the light of Christ. (Candle not shown.)

Note: Lutherans baptize people of all ages— not just infants.

After the baptism in water and God's word, the pastor traces the cross on the baptized person's forehead, often with anointing oil, and declares that he or she now belongs to Christ.

When children are baptized, their parents bring them to the font and make important promises to bring the child up in the Christian faith.

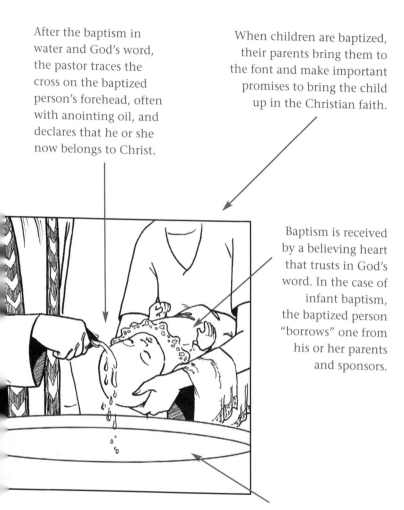

Baptism is received by a believing heart that trusts in God's word. In the case of infant baptism, the baptized person "borrows" one from his or her parents and sponsors.

Water is the earthly element in baptism. God uses it to wash away sin and to drown the "old Adam" or "old Eve" in the baptized person. Water in itself can't do it— baptism is water connected to the power of God's word, and it is received by God's gift of faith.

HOW TO RECEIVE COMMUNION

The Sacrament of Holy Communion (sometimes called the Lord's Supper, the Eucharist, or simply the Meal) is a central event in Lutheran worship. All five senses are engaged in communion, and it is the most interactive part of the service. Local customs for receiving communion can be confusing or complex, so it's wise to pay attention and prepare.

1 Determine which method of distribution is used.
Verbal directions or printed instructions will likely be given prior to the distribution. The three most common methods for communion are *individual cups*, a *common cup*, or *intinction* (see pages 37–39).

Note: Some congregations commune at "tables" (gathered around the altar), and some practice "continuous communion" with bread and wine stations, and some do both.

2 Look for guidance from the usher.
The usher will direct the people in each row or pew to stand and get in line.

3 Proceed to the communion station.
Best practice is often simply to follow the person in front of you and do what they do.

4 Kneel, if appropriate.
Congregations that commune at "tables" often do so by instructing communicants to kneel at an altar railing. When this happens, remember to stand slowly to avoid jostling your neighbor. Assist people who are elderly with altar rail navigation when they need help.

Individual Cups

❶ Receive the bread.
Extend your hands with palms facing up. After the server places the bread in your open hands, grasp the piece with the fingers of one hand. When the server says, "The body of Christ, given for you," eat the bread.

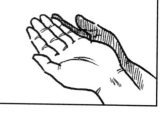

To receive the bread, make a "cross" or "cradle" with your hands, palms up.

Note: Bread is commonly distributed in both baked or "loaf" form and in wafer form. Either is acceptable.

❷ Receive the wine.
Take a filled cup from the tray. Some congregations provide a tray of empty cups as you come forward. If so, take one and hold it out to be filled by the server. When the server says, "The blood of Christ, shed for you," drink the wine.

❸ Return the empty cup.
A communion assistant may follow the servers with a tray for the used cups. Deposit your empty cup. It may be necessary for you to carry the empty cup over to a plate or basket located strategically on the way back to your seat.

Common Cup

① **Receive the bread.**
See previous page.

② **Receive the wine.**
The wine will be served
in a large cup or "chalice,"
as a sign of unity. Assist the
server by placing one hand
underneath the cup and
the other hand on its side.
Help the server guide the
cup to your lips.

③ **Avoid leaving backwash.**
Drink only one sip from
the common cup. Remove
your lips from the cup
immediately after receiving
the wine.

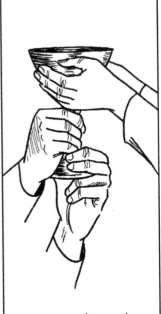

*Use teamwork to receive
the wine by common cup.*

Intinction

Note: The word *intinction*
is from the Latin word
intingere, which means "to dip."

① **Receive the bread.**
Follow the same procedure as with individual cups and
common cup, but DO NOT EAT THE BREAD YET. If you
accidentally eat the bread prematurely, REMAIN CALM.
Simply ask for another piece.

❷ Receive the wine.

Position the bread you are holding over the cup. Grasp the bread tightly and dip just the edge of it into the wine. When the server says, "The blood of Christ shed for you," eat the wine-soaked bread.

❸ Do not panic if you accidentally drop your bread into the cup.

Again, the server can provide you with more bread. If the person distributing bread is too far away, the wine server may allow you to drink directly from the cup. Receiving only one element (bread *or* wine) counts as full participation in communion.

Gently dip the bread in the wine for communion by intinction.

Once You Have Communed

- *Return to your seat.* If communion is distributed in one continuous line, you may immediately return to your pew.

  OR

- *Wait for the completion of the distribution.* If you're being served as a group at the altar rail, you may need to wait until all other worshipers are served before returning to your seat. This is an appropriate time to close your eyes, pray, or listen to the communion music.

- *Receive the post-communion blessing.* When everyone has been served, the presiding minister may bless the group. You may make the sign of the cross during this blessing. (See illustration on page 104.)

- *Continue to participate when seated.* After returning to your place, you may join the congregation in singing the remaining communion hymns, or pray in silence.

Be Aware

- When receiving the bread, place one upward palm on top of the other symbolically to make a "cross" or "cradle" with your hands.

- Many congregations offer the option of grape juice in addition to wine during communion. Verbal or written instructions will be given prior to distribution so you will be able to identify which chalice or cup contains grape juice.

- After receiving the bread and wine, avoid saying, "Thank you" to the server. The body and blood are gifts from God. If you wish, a gentle "Amen" is appropriate.

- Pastoral blessings are often available for children or adults who are not communing.

HOW TO PASS THE PLATE

Passing the offering plate requires physical flexibility and an ability to adapt to differing practices. The offering is a practice that dates back to Old Testament times, linking money and personal finance directly to one's identity as a child of God. Giving of one's financial resources is an integral part of a healthy faith life.

❶ Pay close attention to instructions, if any.
The presiding minister may announce the method of offering, or instructions may be printed in the worship bulletin or projected on an overhead screen.

❷ Be alert for the plate's arrival at your row or pew.
Keep an eye on the ushers, if there are any. In most congregations, guiding and safeguarding the offering plate is their job, so wherever they are, so is the plate. As the plate approaches you, set aside other activity and prepare for passing.

❸ Avoid watching your neighbor or making judgments about their offering.
Many people contribute once a month by mail and some by automatic withdrawal from a bank account. If your neighbor passes the plate to you without placing an envelope, check, or cash in it, do not assume they didn't contribute.

❹ Place your offering in the plate as you pass it politely to the next person.
Do not attempt to make change from the plate if your offering is in cash. Avoid letting the plate rest in your lap as you finish writing a check. Simply pass it on and hand your check to an usher as you leave at the end of worship.

❺ Be sensitive to idiosyncrasies in plate types.
Some congregations use traditional, wide-rimmed, felt-lined, brass-plated offering plates. Some use baskets of varying types. Some use cloth bags hung at the ends of long wooden poles that the ushers extend inward from the ends of the pews.

Three Typical Styles of Offering Plates

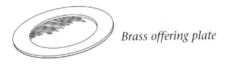
Brass offering plate

Plain offering basket

Offering basket on long pole

Be Aware

- Some congregations place the offering plate or basket at the rear of the worship space.

- Your church offering may be tax deductible, as provided by law. Consider making your offering by check or automatic withdrawal; you will receive a statement from your church in the first quarter of the next year.

- Churches often depend entirely upon the money that comes in through congregational offerings. If you are a member, resolve to work yourself toward tithing as a putting-your-money-where-your-mouth-is expression of faith. (The term *tithing* means "one-tenth" and refers to the practice of giving 10 percent of one's gross income to support the church's work.)

- Everyone, regardless of their age, has something to offer.

- Offerings are not fees or dues given out of obligation. They are gifts of thanksgiving returned to God from the heart.

HOW TO SHARE THE PEACE IN CHURCH

In Romans 16:16, Paul tells members of the congregation to "greet one another with a holy kiss." The First Letter of Peter ends, "Greet one another with a kiss of love. Peace to all of you who are in Christ" (1 Peter 5:14).

Some Lutherans worry about this part of the worship service due to its free-for-all nature. Some also feel uncomfortable because of their fear of being hugged. You can survive the peace, however, with these steps.

❶ Adopt a peaceful frame of mind.
Clear your mind of distracting and disrupting thoughts so you can participate joyfully and reverently.

❷ Determine the appropriate form of safe touch.
Handshaking is most common. Be prepared, however, for hugs, half-hugs, one-armed hugs, pats, and other forms of physical contact. Nods are appropriate for distances greater than two pews or rows.

❸ Refrain from extraneous chitchat.
The sharing of the peace is not the time for lengthy introductions to new people, comments about the weather, or observations about yesterday's game. A brief encounter is appropriate, but save conversations for the coffee hour.

❹ Make appropriate eye contact.
Look the other person in the eye but do not stare. The action of looking the person in the eye highlights the relationship brothers and sisters in Christ have with one another.

Make good eye contact as you share God's peace with others.

❺ Declare the peace of God.

"The peace of the Lord be with you," "Peace be with you," "The peace of God," "God's peace," and "The peace of Christ," are ways of speaking the peace. Once spoken, the peace is there. Move on to the next person.

Be Aware

• Safe touch involves contact that occurs within your personal space but does not cause discomfort or unease.

HOW TO STAY ALERT IN CHURCH

❶ Get adequate sleep.
Late Saturday nights are Sunday morning's worst enemy. Resolve to turn in earlier. A good night's sleep on Friday night is equally important to waking rested on Sunday, as sleep debt builds up over time.

❷ Drink plenty of water, though not too much.
It is easier to remain alert when you are well hydrated. Consider keeping a small bottle of water with you during worship. One quick bathroom break is considered permissible. Two or more are bad form.

❸ Eat a high-protein breakfast.
Foods high in carbohydrates force your body to metabolize them into sugars, which can make you drowsy. If your diet allows, eat foods high in protein instead, such as scrambled eggs with bacon.

❹ Arrive early and find the coffee pot.
If you don't drink coffee, consider a caffeinated soda.

❺ Focus on your posture.
Sit up straight with your feet planted firmly on the floor. Avoid slouching, as this encourages sleepiness. Good posture will promote an alert bearing and assist in paying attention, so you'll get more out of worship.

❻ If you have difficulty focusing on the service, divert your attention. Occupy your mind, not your hands.
Look around the worship space for visual stimuli. Keep your mind active in this way while continuing to listen.

❼ Stay alert by flexing muscle groups in a pattern.
Clench toes and feet; flex calf muscles, thighs, glutei, abdomen, hands, arms, chest, and shoulders. Repeat. Avoid shaking, rocking, or other movements that attract undue attention.

❽ If all else fails, consider pinching yourself.
Dig your nails into the fleshy part of your arm or leg, pinch yourself, bite down on your tongue with moderate pressure. Try not to cry out.

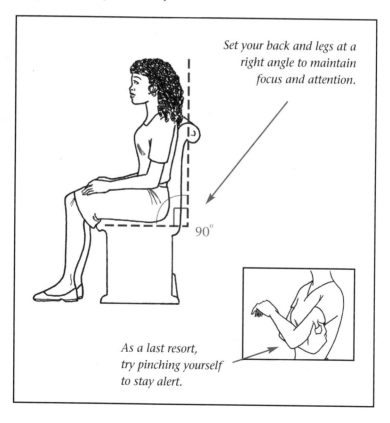

Set your back and legs at a right angle to maintain focus and attention.

90°

As a last resort, try pinching yourself to stay alert.

WHAT TO BRING TO A CHURCH POTLUCK (BY REGION)

It is a generally followed practice in North American churches to enjoy three courses at potlucks (commonly referred to as "dishes"). Many of these dishes take on the flavor of the regions or cultures they represent. For best results, the preparer should understand the context in which the "dish" is presented.

The Salad

Potluck salads are quite different from actual salads. In preparation for making a potluck salad, ask yourself three questions:

- Is this dish mostly meat-free?
- Can this dish be served with a spoon or salad tongs?
- Can it be served chilled?

If the answer is "yes" to any of these questions, consider the dish a potluck-eligible salad.

The Mixture

This is the foundation of any potluck salad. It gives the salad a sense of direction. If at all possible, use ingredients that are indigenous to your area. For example, broccoli, lettuce, apples, macaroni, and candy bars are common in more temperate climates.

The Crunchy Stuff

This component gives life and pizzazz to an otherwise bland salad. Examples: tortilla chips, shoestring potato crisps, onion crisps, and fried pigskins.

The Glue

The glue holds the salad together. The variety of available types is stunning, ranging from a traditional oil-based salad dressing to mayonnaise and non-dairy whipped topping. Use your imagination. Consult regional recipes for exact ingredients.

Note: Some salads are best when made well in advance and allowed to sit overnight. This is called *marinating*, or "controlled decomposition." Do not use actual glue adhesive. Other salads are best prepared immediately before serving.

The Casserole

A three-layered dish, typically. In order to make each casserole as culturally relevant as possible, use the following guidelines. Consult local restaurants for ideas, when in doubt.

Starch

East Coast: pasta or rice pilaf

Midwest: rice, potatoes, noodles, or more rice

South: grits

Southwest: black, red, or pinto beans

West Coast: tofu

Meat

East Coast: sausage or pheasant

Midwest: ground beef—in a pinch, SPAM® luncheon meat

South: crawdad or marlin

Southwest: pulled pork

West Coast: tofu

Cereal

East Coast: corn flakes

Midwest: corn flakes

South: corn flakes

Southwest: corn flakes

West Coast: tofu flakes

Note: The starch and meat may be mixed with a cream-based soup. The cereal must always be placed on the top of the casserole.

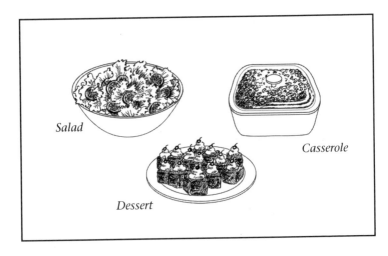

Salad

Casserole

Dessert

The Dessert

The most highly valued dish at a potluck, this can be the simplest and most fun to make. There are two key ingredients:

1. flour
2. fudge

Regional influences can be quite profound. The following are examples of typical desserts around the country. Consult your church's seniors for the nuances of your region.

Cleveland: fudge brownies with fudge frosting

Kansas City: triple-fudge fudge with fudge sauce and a side of fudge

Los Angeles: tofu fudge

Miami: fudge

New York City: cheesecake with fudge drizzle

Be Aware

- Use caution when preparing a dish. Adding local ingredients to any meat, salad, or dessert can increase the fellowship factor of your potluck exponentially. It also raises the risk of a "flop."

- Always follow safe food-handling guidelines.

- Any combination of flavored gelatin, shredded carrots, mini-marshmallows, and canned pears is an acceptable "utility" dish, should you be unable to prepare one from the above categories.

FIVE IMPORTANT THINGS THE LUTHERAN REFORMERS WROTE (OR TRANSLATED) AND WHY THEY'RE STILL IMPORTANT TODAY

① The Augsburg Confession

In 1530, the Holy Roman Emperor called the Lutheran reformers to the city of Augsburg, Germany, to defend their teachings. The document they presented became known as the Augsburg Confession. It is mentioned in every Lutheran congregation's constitution to this day. The Augsburg Confession shows how the reformers talked about God's love for sinners. It also depicts how Lutherans organized themselves to make sure God's promises can be proclaimed.

② The Small and Large Catechisms

Martin Luther led a team of people to see how well congregations were doing making sure people got the good news of Jesus. They found that many Christians in their territories didn't know the most basic parts of the faith. Luther wrote the Small Catechism so families would have a handy summary of the Christian faith. He wrote the Large Catechism so pastors could learn to preach so that people would have faith.

Martin Luther wrote the Catechisms to support people in their daily faith walk.

❸ Luther's "September Testament"

In Luther's time, most people never read the Bible because most copies were written in Latin, a language that no one spoke and few Germans could even read. Luther changed this by translating the New Testament into German. The first edition became known as the "September Testament" because it was printed in September 1522. By translating Scripture into German, Luther returned the New Testament to the language of the people, a process that continues today. No matter what language someone speaks, God's Word can still proclaim freedom in Christ to them.

❹ The Formula of Concord

After Luther died, his German followers argued about what his teachings really meant. For the next 30 years, they fought about how God's law works, whether we have free will, and what happens in the Lord's Supper. They managed to settle these issues and published their agreement: The Formula of Concord. Along with the Augsburg Confession, the Formula of Concord helps the church's preachers and teachers know how to do their work so people can hear what Christ has done for them.

❺ Sermons

Perhaps the most important work the Lutheran reformers did was to change what pastors preached. Martin Luther argued that God's Word had been held captive by bad preaching. By changing preaching to focus on proclaiming the gospel, Luther and the other reformers hoped to make sure God's promises could be freed to inspire people of faith. When that happened, people could actually trust Jesus as their Savior.

Martin Luther nailed his Ninety-five Theses to a church door in Wittenberg, setting the Reformation in motion. One of Luther's main attacks was against the sale of "indulgences," which claimed that people could buy their way into heaven.

SEVEN IMPORTANT THINGS LUTHER SAID (AND ONE FUNNY ONE) AND WHAT THEY MEANT

❶ "When our Lord and Master, Jesus Christ, said, 'Repent,' [Matthew 4:17] he called for the entire life of believers to be one of repentance."

—*Ninety-five Theses* (1517)

Luther meant that faith and its Christly acts of love and service are never to be separated from real life. Faith isn't just a hobby, it's an entire way of life!

❷ "The Law says, 'do this,' and it's never done. Grace says, 'believe in this,' and everything is already done."

—*Heidelberg Disputation* (1518)

This statement highlights how important Martin Luther believed it to be that Christians understand the difference between God's law and the gospel. A life free to serve others begins with this. No matter how well you keep the law, only the free gift of the gospel can save you.

❸ "A Christian is a perfectly free lord of all, subject to none. A Christian is a perfectly dutiful servant of all, subject to all."

—*The Freedom of a Christian* (1520)

By this, Luther meant that Jesus Christ is a Christian's only Lord—a Lord who commands us to love our neighbor as we love ourselves.

❹ "Unless I am convinced by the testimony of the Scriptures or by clear reason ... I am bound by the Scriptures I have quoted and my conscience is captive to the Word of God. I cannot and I will not retract anything, since it is neither safe nor right to go against conscience. I cannot do otherwise, here I stand, may God help me, Amen."

—*Speech at the Diet of Worms* (April 15, 1521)

With this bold and defiant statement, Martin Luther drew a line in the sand and started an age of reformation for the Christian church.

❺ "Be a sinner and sin boldly, but believe and rejoice in Christ even more boldly, for he is victorious over sin, death, and the world."

—*Letter to Philip Melanchthon* (August 1, 1521)

Jesus came to save sinners. There's no point in denying you're a sinner. But more importantly, knowing you're a sinner will bring you closer to Jesus Christ, the one person who can save you from sin and death.

❻ "This is most certainly true."

—*Small Catechism* (1529)

The freedom God declares through Jesus Christ can be fully believed and should not be doubted. Luther wanted the word *Amen* to be spoken with complete confidence.

Martin Luther's last written words.

It's true. We're beggars

❼ "It's true. We're beggars."
—*Luther's last written words* (February 16, 1546)

This is Luther's final testimony to humankind's total dependence on the grace and mercy of God and to life's character as an absolute gift.

❽ "Your manure cure didn't help me either."
—*Letter to Katie Luther* (1537)

Medieval home remedies for skin rashes weren't always what they were cracked up to be. Luther tried one of his wife's, and apparently it didn't work.

FIVE THINGS YOU SHOULD KNOW ABOUT THE LUTHERAN REFORMATION

❶ **Most people in medieval times had low expectations.**
They didn't know anything about advanced medicine, modern psychology, or what it was like to live in a democracy. They didn't expect to live very long. They didn't think they had much power over their lives. And they didn't think being an "individual" was very important.

❷ **The "Lutheran" reformers were Catholic.**
The reformers wanted to make changes within the one Christian church in Europe, but they wanted to stay Catholic. None of them ever expected that their actions would lead to the dozens of Christian denominations around today.

❸ **People in medieval times weren't allowed to choose their own religion.**
You could believe whatever you wanted, but you could only practice the faith your prince or king chose. After the Reformation, only the regions whose princes had signed the Augsburg Confession could practice any faith other than Catholicism.

❹ Martin Luther wasn't the only reformer.
Luther wanted the church to rediscover the good news of Jesus that creates and restores faith. Other reformers fought for these changes: separation of church and state, a mystical relationship with God, better-educated priests, and more moral leaders in the church.

❺ Luther and his colleagues cared about what you hear in church today.
They taught pastors how to tell the difference between law and gospel so the Word of God would hit home and create faith. This skill has been taught to Lutheran pastors ever since.

FIVE FACTS ABOUT LIFE IN MEDIEVAL TIMES

❶ It lasted more than 1,000 years.
By some counts, the medieval period (or Middle Ages) covered an era that began around the year 391 (when Christianity became the Roman Empire's only legal religion) and ended around 1517 (the year Martin Luther wrote the Ninety-five Theses).

❷ Life was nasty, brutish, and short.
People who survived childhood usually did not live long past age 40. If disease or starvation didn't get you, violence and warfare did. It's been estimated that during the 1400s about one-third of Europe's population died of bubonic plague. Sanitation was practically non-existent.

Road travel was harsh and sanitation was minimal during the Middle Ages.

❸ The Christian church grew larger, more influential, and more dominant.

Headquartered in Rome, the Western church became a superpower. Church and state became inseparable. At its height (ca. 1000–1300), "Christian Crusaders" battled with Muslims and others for control of the "Holy Land," Thomas Aquinas wrote his *Summa Theologica*, and hundreds of "heretics" were burned to death.

❹ The "Cult of the Saints" developed.

Over the centuries, a system grew in which the leftover good works (merits) of the saints could be distributed to others, with the pope in charge of this store (treasury) of good works. With his Ninety-five Theses, Luther challenged this system.

❺ Humanist and Renaissance-age thinkers also worked for reform.

At the end of the Middle Ages, early reformers such as Jan Hus and Girolamo Savonarola confronted the church corruptions they saw. Hus was burned, and Savonarola was hanged. For other examples, see "History's Six Most Notorious Heretics" on the next two pages.

HISTORY'S SIX MOST NOTORIOUS HERETICS

Though vilified by those who write history, heretics played a critical role in the church. They refined its message and forced the church to be honest with itself. But heretics usually payed the ultimate price, and often they were wrong.

❶ Hypatia of Alexandria (370–415)
Hypatia was an African philosopher, mathematician, physicist, astronomer, and director of Alexandria's Library, once the largest in the world. Bishop Cyril of Alexandria, out of jealousy, declared her a heretic and ordered her to be tortured and burned at the stake, together with her writings. Her mistakes were to prefer study to marriage, to know more than the bishop, and to be a female teacher of males.

❷ Pelagius (354–418)
Pelagius was a Celtic monk who believed in the goodness of human nature and the freedom of human will. These beliefs led him to denounce the doctrine of original sin—a core tenet of the church—and suggest that human beings were equal participants in their salvation with Jesus Christ. The *Pelagianism* movement, named after him, was a strict teaching of self-reliance. When Pelagius taught that one could achieve grace without the church, he was excommunicated.

❸ Joan of Arc (1412–1431)
Joan was a French peasant girl who was able to hear heavenly voices that urged her to liberate her nation from the British occupation. She was 19 when sentenced as a heretic and burned at the stake. Joan's fault was to be a better army leader than men. She is now a national hero.

❹ Girolamo Savonarola (1452–1498)

His parents wanted him to be a physician, but this Italian youngster decided to be a Dominican monk and serve people who were poor. He preached against Pope Alexander VI and the powerful Medici family. Members of the wealthy church and society hung and burned him, then threw his ashes in the Arnos River to prevent him from having a restful place.

❺ Martin Luther (1483–1546)

His father, a peasant and coal miner, wanted him to be a lawyer. Martin disappointed him and became an Augustinian monk. Emperor Charles V and Pope Leo X threw him out of the church and put a price on his head, but Luther continued serving the poor, preaching and living the Bible, and sharing hospitality at the family dinner table.

❻ Hatuey (?–1511)

This Native American leader from the Guahaba region escaped from Haiti to Cuba. The brave Hatuey was captured and declared a heretic. A priest wanted to baptize him in order for the Indian to get to heaven after being burnt. The Taíno chief rejected the Christian rite when he heard that in heaven there would also be people from Spain.

HOW TO AVOID GETTING BURNED AT THE STAKE

Burning at the stake has a centuries-long history as punishment for heretics. (A heretic is someone who challenges established church teachings.) Some historians argue that many heretics have performed an essential function by forcing the church to clarify its position.

Martin Luther himself was declared a heretic by the pope in 1521, when he would not recant his teachings, but he survived under the protection of a friendly prince. While heretics are no longer treated in this way, it is nevertheless good to be prepared.

❶ Avoid public heresy.
Heresy is any formal public statement that disagrees with the church on an issue of dogma. The Lutheran church was founded upon such statements. Martin Luther's Ninety-five Theses, for example, were heretical and entered as evidence at the Diet of Worms in 1521.

Here's what to do if you are accused of heresy:

- Demand an immediate public trial. By this point, your rights may have evaporated. Speak up anyway.

- State your position clearly and repeatedly. Get it on the record in your own words.

- Consider your options. If in a church trial you believe you might change enough minds to ward off execution, consider proceeding.

If accused of heresy, demand an immediate public trial. State your position clearly.

- Support your case with Holy Scripture. In a trial, you will be doomed without sufficient evidence from the Bible, history, and church doctrine.

- If the above steps fail, consider recanting. You could be wrong.

❷ **Avoid practicing witchcraft.**
Witchcraft is considered a form of heresy, since it depends upon powers other than God and the authority of the church. Practicing witchcraft does *not* include wearing Halloween costumes or reading books about wizards.

❸ **Avoid getting nabbed in a political uprising.**
Historically, persons who posed a political threat were sometimes burned at the stake. Or crucified.

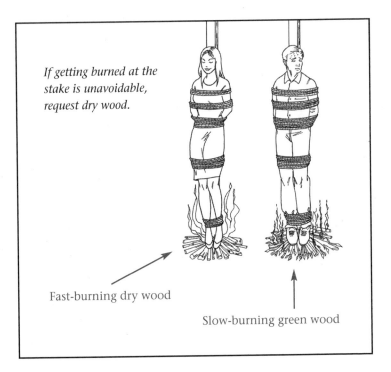

If getting burned at the stake is unavoidable, request dry wood.

Fast-burning dry wood

Slow-burning green wood

Be Aware

- If you find yourself in a situation where being burned at the stake poses an imminent threat, try wearing flame-retardant material.

- If there is no hope of escape, request dry wood and plenty of dry kindling. Green wood burns slower, smokier, and at lower temperatures, causing a more painful death.

WORLD RELIGIONS

Listed by approximate number of adherents:

Christianity	2 billion
Islam	1.3 billion
Hinduism	900 million
Agnostic/Atheist/Non-Religious	850 million
Buddhism	360 million
Confucianism and Chinese traditional	225 million
Primal-indigenous	150 million
Shinto	108 million
African traditional	95 million
Sikhism	23 million
Juche	19 million
Judaism	14 million
Spiritism	14 million
Baha'i	7 million
Jainism	4 million
Cao Dai	3 million
Tenrikyo	2.4 million
Neo-Paganism	1 million
Unitarian-Universalism	800,000
Rastafarianism	700,000
Scientology	600,000
Zoroastrianism	150,000

COMPARATIVE RELIGIONS

	Baha'i	Buddhism	Christianity
Founder and date founded	Bahá'u'lláh (1817-1892) founded Babism in 1844 from which Baha'i grew.	Founded by Siddhartha Gautama (the Buddha) in Nepal in the 6th-5th centuries B.C.	Founded by Jesus of Nazareth, a Palestinian Jew, in the early 1st century A.D.
Number of adherents in 2000	About 7 million worldwide; 750,000 U.S.	360 million worldwide; 2 million U.S.	About 2 billion worldwide; 160 million U.S.
Main tenets	The oneness of God, the oneness of humanity, and the common foundation of all religion. Also, equality of men and women, universal education, world peace, and a world federal government.	Meditation and the practice of virtuous and moral behavior can lead to Nirvana, the state of enlightenment. Before that, one is subjected to repeated lifetimes, based on behavior.	Jesus is the Son of God and God in human form. In his death and resurrection, he redeems humanity from sin and gives believers eternal life. His teachings frame the godly life for his followers.
Sacred or primary writing	Bahá'u'lláh's teachings, along with those of the Bab, are collected and published.	The Buddha's teachings and wisdom are collected and published.	The Bible is a collection of Jewish and Near Eastern writings spanning some 1,400 years.

Confucianism	Hinduism	Islam	Judaism
Founded by the Chinese philosopher Confucius in the 6th-5th centuries B.C. One of several traditional Chinese religions.	Developed in the 2nd century B.C. from indigenous religions in India, and later combined with other religions, such as Vaishnavism.	Founded by the prophet Muhammad ca. A.D. 610. The word *Islam* is Arabic for "submission to God."	Founded by Abraham, Isaac, and Jacob ca. 2000 B.C.
6 million worldwide (does not include other traditional Chinese beliefs); U.S. uncertain.	900 million worldwide; 950,000 U.S.	1.3 billion worldwide; 5.6 million U.S.	14 million worldwide; 5.5 million U.S.
Confucius's followers wrote down his sayings or *Analects*. They stress relationships between individuals, families, and society based on proper behavior and sympathy.	Hinduism is based on a broad system of sects. The goal is release from repeated reincarnation through yoga, adherence to the Vedic scriptures, and devotion to a personal guru.	Followers worship Allah through the Five Pillars. Muslims who die believing in God, and that Muhammad is God's messenger, will enter Paradise.	Judaism holds the belief in a monotheistic God, whose Word is revealed in the Hebrew Bible, especially the Torah. Jews await the coming of a messiah to restore creation.
Confucius's *Analects* are collected and still published.	The Hindu scriptures and Vedic texts.	The Koran is a collection of Muhammad's writings.	The Hebrew scriptures compose the Christian Old Testament.

FAMILY TREE OF CHRISTIANITY

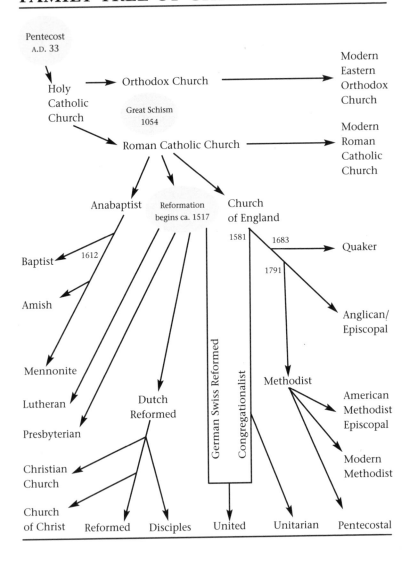

U.S. CHRISTIAN DENOMINATIONS

Listed by approximate number of adult adherents:

Catholic	60 million
Baptist	30 million
Methodist/Wesleyan	13 million
Lutheran	9 million
Pentecostal/Charismatic	5 million
Orthodox	4 million
Presbyterian	4 million
Episcopalian/Anglican	3 million
Churches of Christ	3 million
Congregational/ United Church of Christ	2 million
Assemblies of God	1 million
Anabaptist	600,000
Adventist	100,000

COMPARATIVE DENOMINATIONS:

	Lutheran	Catholic	Orthodox
Founded when and by whom?	1517: Martin Luther challenges Catholic teachings with his Ninety-five Theses. 1530: the Augsburg Confession is published.	Catholics consider Jesus' disciple Peter (died ca. A.D. 66) the first pope. Through Gregory the Great (540-604), papacy is firmly established.	A.D 330: Emperor Constantine renames Byzantium "Constantinople" and declares Christianity the empire's religion.
Adherents in 2000?	About 60 million worldwide; about 9 million U.S.	About 1 billion worldwide; 60 million U.S.	About 225 million worldwide; about 4 million U.S.
How is Scripture viewed?	Protestant canon contains 39 OT books, 27 NT. Scripture alone is the authoritative witness to the gospel.	The canon is 46 books in the OT (Apocryhpha included) and 27 in the NT. Interpretation is subject to church tradition.	49 OT books (Catholic plus three more) and 27 NT. Scripture is subject to tradition.
How are we saved?	We are saved by grace when God grants righteousness through faith alone. Good works inevitably result, but they are not the basis of salvation.	God infuses the gift of faith in the baptized, which is maintained by good works and receiving Penance and the Eucharist.	God became human so humans could be deified, that is, have the energy of God's life in them.
What is the church?	The congregation of believers, mixed with the lost, in which the gospel is preached and the sacraments are administered.	The mystical body of Christ, who established it with the pope as its head; he pronounces doctrine infallibly.	The body of Christ in unbroken historical connection with the apostles; the Roman pope is one of many patriarchs who govern.
What about the sacraments?	Baptism is necessary for salvation. The Lord's Supper is bread & wine that, with God's Word are truly Jesus' body & blood.	Catholics hold seven sacraments. Baptism removes original sin; usually infants. The Eucharist undergoes transubstantiation.	Baptism initiates God's life in the baptized; adults and children. In the Eucharist, bread & wine are changed into body & blood.

Liturgical Churches

	Anglican	Presbyterian	Methodist
Founded when and by whom?	1534: Henry VIII is declared head of the Church of England. 1549: Thomas Cranmer produces the first *Book of Common Prayer*.	1536: John Calvin writes *Institutes of the Christian Religion*. 1789: Presbyterian Church U.S.A. is organized.	1738: Anglican ministers John and Charles Wesley convert. 1784: U.S. Methodists form a separate church body.
Adherents in 2000?	45-75 million worldwide; about 3 million U.S.	40-48 million worldwide; 4 million U.S.	20-40 million worldwide; about 13 million U.S.
How is Scripture viewed?	Protestant canon accepted. Scripture is interpreted in light of tradition and reason.	Protestant canon accepted. Scripture is "witness without parallel" to Christ, but in human words reflecting beliefs of the time.	Protestant canon accepted. Scripture is primary source for Christian doctrine.
How are we saved?	We share in Christ's victory, who died for our sins, freeing us through baptism to become living members of the church.	We are saved by grace alone. Good works result, but are not the basis of salvation.	We are saved by grace alone. Good works must result, but do not obtain salvation.
What is the church?	The body of Christ is based on "apostolic succession" of bishops, going back to the apostles. In the U.S., it is the Episcopal Church.	The body of Christ includes all of God's chosen and is represented by the visible church. Governed by regional "presbyteries" of elders.	The body of Christ, represented by church institutions. Bishops oversee regions and appoint pastors, who are itinerant.
What about the sacraments?	Baptism brings infant and convert initiates into the church; in Communion, Christ's body & blood are truly present.	Baptism is not necessary for salvation. The Lord's Supper is Christ's body & blood, which are spiritually present to believers.	Baptism is a sign of regeneration; in the Lord's Supper, Jesus is really present.

COMPARATIVE DENOMINATIONS:

	Anabaptist	Congregational	Baptist
Founded when and by whom?	1523: Protestants in Zurich, Switzerland, begin believers' baptism. 1537: Menno Simons begins Mennonite movement.	1607: Members of England's illegal "house church" exiled. 1620: Congregationalists arrive in the New World on the *Mayflower*.	1612: John Smythe and other Puritans form the first Baptist church. 1639: The first Baptist church in America is established.
Adherents in 2000?	About 2 million worldwide; about 600,000 U.S.	More than 2 million worldwide; about 2 million U.S.	100 million worldwide; about 30 million U.S.
How is Scripture viewed?	Protestant canon accepted. Scripture is inspired but not infallible. Jesus is living Word; Scripture is written Word.	Protestant canon accepted. Bible is the authoritative witness to the Word of God.	Protestant canon accepted. Scripture is inspired and without error; the sole rule of faith.
How are we saved?	Salvation is a personal experience. Through faith in Jesus, we become at peace with God, moving us to follow Jesus' example by being peacemakers.	God promises forgiveness and grace to save "from sin and aimlessness" all who trust him, who accept his call to serve the whole human family.	Salvation is offered freely to all who accept Jesus as Saviour. There is no salvation apart from personal faith in Christ.
What is the church?	The body of Christ, the assembly and society of believers. No one system of government is recognized.	The people of God living as Jesus' disciples. Each local church is self-governing and chooses its own ministers.	The body of Christ; the redeemed throughout history. The term *church* usually refers to local congregations, which are autonomous.
What about the sacraments?	Baptism is for believers only. The Lord's Supper is a memorial of his death.	Congregations may practice infant baptism or believers' baptism or both. Sacraments are symbols.	Baptism is immersion of believers, only as a symbol. The Lord's Supper is symbolic.

Non-Liturgical Churches

	Churches of Christ	Adventist	Pentecostal
Founded when and by whom?	1801: Barton Stone holds Cane Ridge Revival in Kentucky. 1832: Stone's Christians unite with Disciples of Christ.	1844: William Miller's prediction of Christ's return that year failed. 1863: Seventh-Day Adventist Church is organized.	1901: Kansas college students speak in tongues. 1906: Azusa Street revival in L.A. launches movement. 1914: Assemblies of God organized.
Adherents in 2000?	5-6 million worldwide; about 3 million U.S.	About 11 million worldwide; about 100,000 U.S.	About 500 million worldwide; about 5 million U.S.
How is Scripture viewed?	Protestant canon accepted. Scripture is the Word of God. Disciples of Christ view it as a witness to Christ, but fallible.	Protestant canon accepted. Scripture is inspired and without error; Ellen G. White, an early leader, was a prophet.	Protestant canon accepted. Scripture is inspired and without error. Some leaders are considered prophets.
How are we saved?	We must hear the gospel, repent, confess Christ, and be baptized. Disciples of Christ: God saves people by grace.	We repent by believing in Christ as Example (in his life) and Substitute (by his death). Those who are found right with God will be saved.	We are saved by God's grace through Jesus, resulting in our being born again in the Spirit, as evidenced by a life of holiness.
What is the church?	The assembly of those who have responded rightly to the gospel; it must be called only by the name of Christ.	Includes all who believe in Christ. The last days are a time of apostasy, when a remnant keeps God's commandments faithfully.	The body of Christ, in which the Holy Spirit dwells; the agency for bringing the gospel of salvation to the whole world.
What about the sacraments?	Baptism is the immersion of believers only, as the initial act of obedience to the gospel. The Lord's Supper is a symbolic memorial.	Baptism is the immersion of believers only. Baptism and the Lord's Supper are symbolic only.	Baptism is immersion of believers only. A further "baptism in the Holy Spirit" is offered. Lord's Supper is symbolic.

THE SEASONS OF THE CHURCH YEAR AND WHAT THEY MEAN

Advent is a season of longing and anticipation, during which we prepare for the coming of Jesus. The church year begins with Advent, as life begins with birth, starting four Sundays before Christmas. The liturgical color for Advent is blue, which symbolizes waiting and hope.

Christmas is a day *and* a season when we celebrate God's coming among us as a human child: Jesus, Emmanuel (which means "God with us"). The liturgical color for Christmas is white, which reminds us that Jesus is the Light of the world. Christmas lasts for 12 days, from December 25 to January 5.

Epiphany is celebrated on January 6, when we remember the three Wise Men's visit to the Christ child. The color for Epiphany Day is white. During the time after Epiphany we hear stories about Jesus' baptism and early ministry. The color for these Sundays is sometimes white and sometimes green. On the last Sunday we celebrate the Transfiguration. The color for this day is white, and we hear the story of Jesus shining brightly on the mountaintop.

Lent is a season when we turn toward God and think about how our lives need to change. This is also a time to remember our baptism, and how that gift gives us a new start every day! The color for Lent is purple, symbolizing repentance. Lent begins on Ash Wednesday and lasts for 40 days (not including Sundays) and ends on the Saturday before Easter Sunday.

The Three Days are the most important part of the Christian calendar because they mark Jesus' last days, death, and resurrection. These days (approximately three 24-hour periods) begin on Maundy Thursday evening and conclude on Easter evening. On *Maundy Thursday* we hear the story of Jesus' last meal with his disciples and his act of service and love in washing their feet. On *Good Friday* we hear of Jesus' trial, crucifixion, death, and burial. On *Saturday*, at the nighttime *Easter Vigil*, we hear stories about the amazing things God has done for us. It is a night of light, Scripture readings, baptismal remembrance, and communion—the greatest night of the year for Christians. On *Easter Sunday* we celebrate Jesus' resurrection and our new lives in Christ. Easter falls on a different date each year—sometime between March 22 and April 25.

Easter is not just one day, but a whole season when we celebrate the resurrected Jesus. The season begins on Easter Sunday and lasts for 50 days (including Sundays). The color is white, symbolizing resurrection and joy. The Day of Pentecost falls on the 50th day of the season (*Pentecost* means 50th), when we honor the Holy Spirit and the church's mission in the world. This day uses the fiery color of red.

Time after Pentecost is the longest season in the church calendar, lasting almost half the year. Sometimes this is called "ordinary time" because there aren't many special celebrations during these weeks. The liturgical color for the time after Pentecost is green, representing life and growth. Each week we hear a different story about Jesus' ministry from one of the four Gospels.

Special festivals are celebrated throughout the year. Some festivals occur the same time every year, such as Reformation Sunday (last Sunday in October) and All Saints Sunday (first Sunday in November). Others, like saints' days, we might celebrate only when their day falls on a Sunday. The color for these days is either white or red.

THE SEASONS OF THE CHURCH YEAR

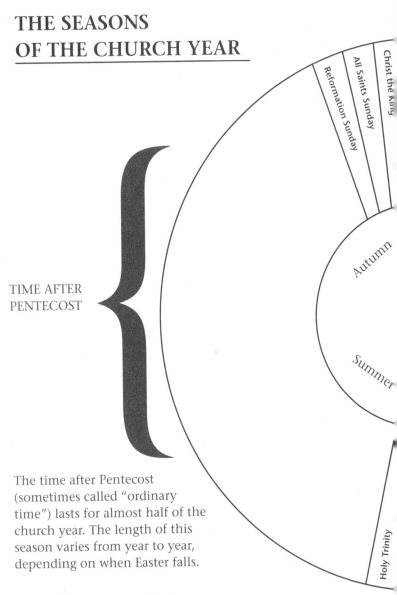

TIME AFTER
PENTECOST

The time after Pentecost
(sometimes called "ordinary
time") lasts for almost half of the
church year. The length of this
season varies from year to year,
depending on when Easter falls.

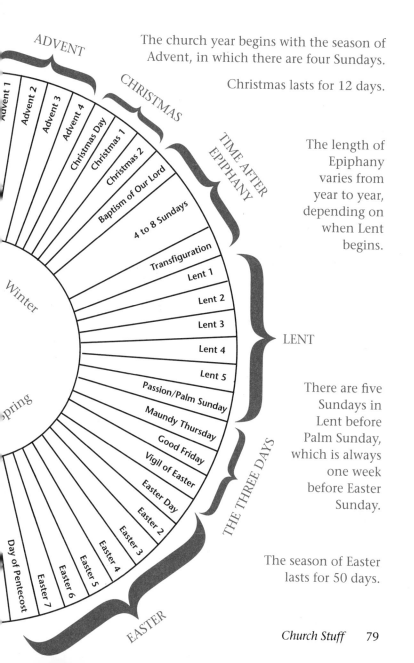

The church year begins with the season of Advent, in which there are four Sundays.

Christmas lasts for 12 days.

The length of Epiphany varies from year to year, depending on when Lent begins.

LENT

There are five Sundays in Lent before Palm Sunday, which is always one week before Easter Sunday.

The season of Easter lasts for 50 days.

MARTIN LUTHER

Lutherans and non-Lutherans alike credit Martin Luther (1483–1546) for spearheading the Reformation by raising important questions about the church and translating the Bible for everyday people.

LUTHER'S GERMANY

Martin Luther was born in the town of Eisleben on November 10, 1483. He received his doctor of theology from the University of Wittenberg, where he taught from 1508 to 1546. In 1530, the Lutheran Reformers traveled to the city of Augsburg to defend their teachings to the Holy Roman Emperor. Luther died in Eisleben on February 18, 1546.

LUTHER'S SEAL

Martin Luther sent the following letter from
Coburg Castle to Lazarus Spengler on July 8, 1530:

Since you wish to know whether my seal is well done, I shall
gladly comply with your request by communicating to you
the thoughts I originally desired my seal to embrace as
indicative of my theology.

First there is a cross, black on a heart in red, as its natural
color. This is to remind me that faith in the Crucified saves
us: for if one believes with the heart, one is justified. Now
although it is a black cross, although it mortifies and is
designed to inflict pain, it nonetheless allows the heart to
keep its color, it does not destroy its nature, that is, it does
not kill but keeps alive. (For the just lives by faith, but faith
in the Crucified.)

Such a heart is to be
centered on a white rose
in order to indicate
that faith yields joy,
comfort, and peace
and straightway
beds one on a white,
pleasing rose. Nor
does faith yield the
peace and joy of the
world. Therefore the
rose would be white and
not red, because white is the
color of the spirits and of all
the angels.

This rose is on a field tinted with the hues of heaven to indicate that this joy in the spirit and faith is a beginning of the future heavenly joy, a joy which, to be sure, is even now present in faith and embraced by hope but is not yet revealed.

And around this field runs a ring of gold to show that the blessedness of heaven endures forever and ever and is more precious than all pleasures and possessions of earth, as gold is the most precious and the noblest metal.

EVERYDAY STUFF

Believing in God involves more than going to church and reading the Bible. It's about keeping your faith with you in every part of your life.

This section includes:

- Advice for helping people in times of trouble.

- Tips on forgiving others and treating them with respect—even if you don't always feel like it.

- Suggestions for avoiding temptation on a daily basis. Some of these ideas go back to the Middle Ages.

HOW TO TELL THE DIFFERENCE BETWEEN THE LAW AND THE GOSPEL

Discerning law from gospel is a critical skill for Christians and the hallmark of Lutheranism. Law and gospel are always connected to God's word. God brings them to you in the Bible, in preaching, in the sacraments, and in all kinds of daily activity. If you listen closely, you'll hear God speaking both law and gospel.

The Law

Martin Luther suggested that the law has two uses: First, to point out and condemn sin. Second, to drive the sinner toward the grace and mercy revealed in Jesus Christ and his cross.

❶ **Listen for the "should."**
God uses the law to tell us what we ought to do so we maintain an orderly, peaceful, and secure world. It therefore always sounds like a demand. Words such as *should*, *ought to*, *must, have to*, and *shall* are a dead giveaway that the law is around somewhere.

❷ **Listen for the First Commandment.**
"You shall have no other gods," is what all other law rises from. The law's goal is to force sinners to act as though God's will is more important than our own.

❸ **Discern who's in charge.**
Demands always require you to do something to fulfill them. If you're being urged to act a certain way to make something happen, it's the law talking.

❹ Be alert to death lurking in the shadows.
When you feel like the demands of life are just about killing you, you can be pretty sure it's God's law nipping at your heels.

The Gospel

❶ Listen for the promise.
If what you're hearing tells you what Christ promises you—without any action on your part—then the gospel is present.

❷ Expect a radical surprise from Jesus.
We sinners should never expect the good news; we should only expect God's judgment. Instead, the gospel brings sinners mercy and life from Jesus.

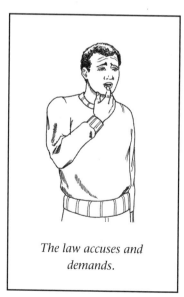

The law accuses and demands.

The gospel liberates and frees us.

❸ Listen for the "for you."

The gospel is always spoken directly to sinners. If what you hear doesn't use the word *you*, it could be a good description about God or Jesus, but it's not quite the gospel. The gospel says it straight out: "You are forgiven." "Jesus died for you."

❹ Remember the promise.

When God's word has changed you, you'll see God's faithfulness in spite of the injustice in the world. When it has caused you to trust God, even though the world says you're a loser, then you can be sure you've heard the gospel.

Be Aware

- Law and gospel can't be defined strictly. They are the *ways* we experience the following two things:

  1. God is working continually to confront and put to death the "you" that turns away and puts your trust in other things. When the law does its work, that's what God is doing.

  2. God is also working continually to create a new faithful person in you. When the gospel does its work, that's what God is doing.

- God sometimes does only the first thing, but God never brings the gospel without the law being present first. It's only when the law stops us from thinking we can make life work out on our own that we become open to hearing God's promises.

HOW TO SHARE YOUR FAITH WITH SOMEONE

Sharing the gospel with others is a natural part of exercising a mature faith. In fact, Jesus commanded his followers to do this, making it an important part of the life of faith (Matthew 28:18-20). Still, Lutherans tend to be rather shy evangelists.

While *evangelism* has become a negative word for some people, sharing the story of salvation in Jesus Christ is still the most rewarding way to live out one's faith. It is also a discipline that takes practice.

❶ Look for the opening.
Regular daily conversations offer lots of chances to talk about your faith. Listen for open-ended comments, such as, "I wonder why life is like that," or, "Sometimes life seems so hard." When possible, offer a response from a Christian perspective. Begin sentences with phrases such as, "I've come to think ..." or, "I don't have the perfect answer, but I believe ..."

❷ Be yourself.
Expressing your faith should be natural and the same as other types of daily conversation. Avoid suddenly switching your tone of voice or vocabulary. Also, don't try to impress the other person with your knowledge. Allow the Holy Spirit to guide you.

❸ Watch for a chance to take the conversation deeper.
Carefully gauge the other person's response. Observe his or her facial expression, verbal tone, and body language. If he or she seems to be closing down, set the topic aside and wait for another time. If he or she keys in and perks up, be prepared to continue.

❹ Open up.
Human beings are attracted to each other by our strengths, but we bond because of our weaknesses. Key to sharing your faith is the willingness to be honest about your own life's struggles. This will communicate safety, which for many people is critical.

❺ Follow up.
Offer to continue the conversation later and arrange a time. At this point, the conversation will have become personally valuable to you. Allowing the person to see your commitment to your faith alongside your continuing questions will reassure him or her of your sincerity.

❻ Offer to share your faith community with the other person.
Most people join a church after being invited by a friend. When the time is right, invite the person to attend with you. Tell the person what makes it special to you.

❼ Try to maintain the relationship regardless of what the person does.
Be prepared for the other person to shut down around faith talk, decline your invitation to attend church, or even appear to avoid you. The most effective way to communicate that you're a follower of Jesus Christ is through your actions; continue to live naturally and with integrity. Watch for another opportunity to open the subject later on.

HOW TO PRAY

Prayer is intimate communication with God and can be used before a meal, at bedtime, during a worship service, or any time the need or opportunity arises. Silent and spoken prayers are both okay and may be used liberally throughout the day. Prayer is also taking time to listen to what God is saying to us. Spontaneous prayer is often best, but the following process may help build the habit.

❶ Assess your need for prayer.
Take stock of the situation at hand, including your motivations. What are you praying *for* and why?

❷ Select a type of prayer.
Prayers of *supplication* (requests for God's help), *contrition* (in which sin is confessed and forgiveness requested), *intercession* (on behalf of others), and others are good and time tested. Books of personal prayers, hymnals, and devotionals often contain helpful, prewritten prayers. Consider also an ad-libbed prayer from the heart.

❸ Select a physical prayer posture.
Many postures are appropriate:

- The most common type of prayer in the New Testament is from a prone position, lying face-down on the ground, arms spread.

- Kneeling with your face and palms upturned is good for prayers of supplication.

- Bowed head with closed eyes and hands folded is common today and aids concentration.

There is no "official" posture for prayer. Choose your posture according to your individual prayer needs.

Choose a comfortable and appropriate prayer posture for your prayer time.

❹ Offer your prayer.
Pray with confidence. God listens to all prayer and responds. Breathe deeply, relax, and be open as the Spirit leads you.

❺ Listen.
Take time during your prayer simply to listen. Some prayer traditions involve only silent meditation as a means of listening for God's voice.

Be Aware

- God hears every prayer.
- Prayer can be done either alone or in the company of others (corporately).
- Environment matters. If possible, consider lighting a candle and dimming the lights to set the correct mood and help block out distractions.

HOW TO WORK FOR PEACE AND JUSTICE ON BEHALF OF PEOPLE WHO ARE POOR AND OPPRESSED

Knowing that good works are the result—not the cause—of salvation, Lutherans have a long and extraordinary record of working for economic justice and relief around the world. Lutheran World Relief, for example, ranks among the world's most powerful aid organizations, often responding faster, longer, and with larger resources than other groups.

Lutheran congregations around the globe also set justice as one of their highest priorities, giving time and money both locally and globally. As followers of Jesus Christ, each individual Christian is linked to Jesus' compassion for people who are poor and called to work tirelessly on their behalf, as he did.

❶ Include people who are poor and oppressed in your daily prayers.

Keeping the needs of others in mind, especially people who suffer as a result of economic inequality, political oppression, or natural disaster, defines a person's good works. Name specific situations in your prayers, and use specific place names and people's names whenever possible. Keep the newspaper on your lap as you pray, if necessary.

❷ Include people who are poor and oppressed in your personal or household budget.

Dedicate some of your personal giving to economic-aid organizations. This should include your congregation. If you already tithe (give 10 percent of your income to your church), consider earmarking a percentage of that money to go directly to relief organizations through your church's budget.

❸ Pay close attention to economic and political conditions in other nations.

You can't help if you don't know what's really going on. Resolve to be a well-informed person who tests the worldview in the news against the worldview in the Bible. Utilize the Internet to locate independent and alternative news sources with unique, on-the-spot perspectives.

❹ Get to know organizations that work for justice locally.

Your congregation probably already organizes to do justice work in your neighborhood. If not, consider taking responsibility to organize a ministry team in your church.

❺ Make working for justice part of your weekly or monthly routine.

Devote a portion of your time regularly to a specific activity that personally connects you to people who are poor and disenfranchised. There is no substitute for personal contact.

6 Vote your conscience.

If you are of voting age, remember that nations will be judged by the way they treat people who are disadvantaged. Keep this in mind when you go to your polling place.

7 Advocate for a cause in which you believe, one that has meaning for you personally.

HOW TO IDENTIFY
A GENUINE MIRACLE

The term *miracle* describes something that causes wonder.
It is usually used in reference to an event that defies logical
explanation and appears to be the work of a higher force,
suggesting a reality beyond the five senses.

❶ Disregard most minor situations.
   The facts should indicate a situation of high order, such
   as one that is life threatening, one involving suffering,
   or involving an immediate threat. Finding your lost keys
   does not necessarily constitute a miracle.

❷ Look for a lack of predictability.
   A positive outcome should be needed and wanted, but
   not expected. Miracles tend to occur "out of the blue"
   rather than as the result of an earthly cause, especially
   a human one.

❸ Evaluate the outcome.
   Miracles achieve a life-giving purpose; they never occur
   outside the will of God. Suffering is relieved, God is
   glorified, Jesus' presence is made manifest, the lowly are
   lifted up, evil is thwarted, creation is revealed, or life is
   saved. The outcome *must* be regarded as good, according
   to biblical standards.

❹ Look for a divine agency.
The ability to make a miracle happen, to guarantee the results, or to take credit for it is beyond human. Often, the event will defy what we know to be true about the laws of nature or probability. If anyone stands to make money or advance an agenda from an event, it is most likely not a miracle.

❺ Adopt a wait-and-see perspective.
A miracle will still be a miracle later on. Labeling something a miracle too quickly could lead down unhelpful paths, while waiting to make the call—pondering the event in your heart—will enhance your faith journey.

Be Aware

- The most overlooked miracle is that God shows up in everyday life events and in such ordinary forms as bread, wine, water, words, and people.

- The miracle of life in Jesus Christ is a daily event and should be regarded as a free gift.

THREE ESSENTIAL PERSONAL SPIRITUAL RITUALS

A spiritual ritual is a routine for building one's faith. Ritual involves action, words, and often images that work together to center one's daily life in Jesus Christ. Medical studies show that people who pray regularly throughout the day suffer less stress, have lower incidence of heart disease, and live longer on average than those who do not.

❶ Morning Devotions

- Directly upon awakening, turn your attention first to God. The silence and solitude available in the morning hours are ideal. (See Luther's Morning Blessing on page 224.)

- Try to make prayer the first activity of your day. If necessary, set your alarm to sound 15 minutes early to give yourself time.

- Begin with thanks and by remembering God's constant presence.

- Identify events you anticipate in your day and how you feel about them.

- Ask God to provide what you need for the day.

- Pray on behalf of other people. Consider keeping a list of names tucked inside your Bible or devotional book.

❷ Mealtime Grace

Human beings naturally pause before a meal. Use those moments to give thanks.

- Consider establishing mealtime grace as a household ritual.

- When eating in public, be considerate of others, but do not abandon your ritual.

- Once your meal is assembled and ready to eat, take time before praying to gather your thoughts and call an appropriate prayer to mind.

Praying before mealtime is a great personal ritual that can be shared with others.

- Many people pray a rote or memorized prayer at mealtimes. Consider occasionally departing from your regular prayer with an extemporaneous one.

❸ Evening Prayer

The other daily rituals you perform in the evening, like brushing your teeth or letting the cat out, create a natural structure for evening prayer.

- Establish a regular time, such as sunset or at bedtime, and commit to it.

- Confess wrongdoing and ask for forgiveness.

- Tell God about the joys and sorrows of the day. Ask for help with the sorrows and give thanks for the joys.

- Identify the good things about the day. On bad days, find at least one thing to give thanks for.

- Consider using a devotional as a guide and companion. (See Luther's Evening Blessing on page 225.)

- Think about involving other members of your household in this ritual. Evening prayer particularly can be enhanced through sharing. When children are included, trace the cross on their foreheads and say a brief blessing as part of the ritual. (See illustration on page 117.)

HOW TO FORGIVE SOMEONE

Forgiving is one of the most difficult disciplines of faith, since it seems to cost you something additional when you've already been wronged. Swallowing your pride and seeking a greater good, however, can yield great healing and growth.

❶ Acknowledge that God forgives you.
When you realize that God has already shown forgiveness, and continues to forgive sinners like you, it's easier to forgive someone else.

❷ Consult Scripture.
Jesus taught the Lord's Prayer to his disciples, who were hungry to become like he was. Forgiveness was a big part of this. Read Matthew 6:9-15.

❸ Seek the person out whenever possible.
Consciously decide to deliver your forgiveness in person. In cases where this is geographically impossible, find an appropriate alternative means, such as the telephone.

Note: This may not be wise in all cases, given the timing of the situation or the level of hurt. Certain problems can be made worse by an unwelcome declaration of forgiveness. Consult with a clergyperson before taking questionable action.

❹ Say, "I forgive you," out loud.
A verbal declaration of forgiveness is ideal. Speaking the words enacts a physical chain reaction that can create healing for both speaker and hearer. In the Bible, Jesus used these words to heal a paralyzed man from across a room.

❺ Pray for the power to forgive.
Praying for this is always good, whether a forgiveness situation is at hand or not. It is especially helpful in cases where declaring forgiveness seems beyond your reach.

Be Aware

• When someone sins against you personally, forgiving them does NOT depend upon them feeling sorry (showing contrition) or asking for your forgiveness. But it helps. You may have to struggle, however, to forgive them without their consent or participation.

HOW TO CONFESS YOUR SINS AND RECEIVE FORGIVENESS

Confession is an "office of the keys" belonging to all baptized persons, that is, anyone may confess and any believer may pronounce the word of forgiveness. A declaration of forgiveness is permanent and binding because it comes from Jesus Christ himself.

❶ Make a mental list of your offenses.

❷ Locate a fellow Christian.
When appropriate, confess your sins to another person.

❸ Resolve to confess of your own free will.
Don't confess merely because someone else wants you to do it. Make your confession voluntarily.

❹ Make your confession fearlessly, aloud if possible.
Confess the sins that burden you, and then confess the sins of which you are not aware or can't remember.

❺ Avoid making up sins.
More important than the facts and figures is a spirit of repentance in your heart.

❻ Receive forgiveness as it is given, in the name of the Father and of the Son and of the Holy Spirit.
God forgives you fully. Make the sign of the cross to help you remember.

❼ Resolve to live joyfully and penitently.
With absolution comes new life in the freedom of God's grace. See "Individual Confession and Forgiveness" on page 218.

Be Aware

- Unburdening your conscience through confession is cleansing and good for the soul; it's not meant to be torture.

- Ultimately, forgiveness comes from God. A perfect and pure confession is not a strict requirement to receive it.

How to Make the Sign of the Cross

Step 1

Step 2

Step 3

Step 4

HOW TO DEFEND YOUR FAITH AGAINST ATTACK

Defending your faith from attack involves tact and savvy, that is, the ability to empathize with your adversary and use his or her affronts creatively without getting baited into an angry or hostile response. The Lutheran theological perspective was hammered out in a context of debate and controversy, though you probably don't need to go looking for a fight nowadays. Just be ready. There is no substitute for knowing your stuff.

1 Employ the 80/20 rule.
In any debate, it is best to listen at least 80 percent of the time and talk 20 percent of the time.

2 Engage in empathic listening.
Empathic listening means to try to comprehend not just the content of the other person's position, but also the emotional thrust behind it. This is important especially in cases where the speaker's emotional expressions are intense.

3 Restate your adversary's argument empathetically.
Use sentences like, "So, you're upset because Christians seem to say one thing and do another."

4 Identify with what the speaker is saying.
For example, say, "I know what you mean. I see a lot of phony behavior at my own church." This elevates the conversation and keeps it civil.

❺ Do your best to put the speaker at ease.
Having made clear that you understand his or her position, you are free to state your defense or counter-point. Offer "I statement" responses, such as, "I wonder how I would stand up under that kind of scrutiny, myself," or, "I do my best not to judge others too harshly. I'd hate to be judged by those standards."

❻ Keep it as upbeat as possible.
Use humility, humor, and a pleasant nature to defuse any tension. Though hard to practice, it is possible to disagree with someone while remaining friends.

❼ Give your opponent his or her due.
When the speaker makes a good argument, say, "You make a good point." This will further elevate the conversation. If you still disagree, make your counter-argument calmly.

❽ Avoid closing off the conversation or leaving it on a sour note.
If you can, offer to continue the discussion over a lunch that you buy. Avoid falling into a "winner take all" mind-set. Keep respect as your highest value.

Be Aware

- Attacks on faith are not limited to verbal assaults, especially in countries such as China or Vietnam, where religious persecution is a reality. Take care when visiting such places, especially when distributing religious materials or sharing stories about your faith.

- It is best in all cases to avoid sounding smug or preachy where your points resemble counterattacks.

HOW TO RESIST TEMPTATION

Lutherans have inherited lots of good advice from Martin Luther. One thing we've lost is the down-to-earth, common sense ways that Luther advised people to resist temptation. These are ideas he gave people who said they were tempted.

❶ Run the opposite direction.
Learn to identify the things that tempt you and avoid situations in which temptation will occur. When you see a temptation coming down the road, take a detour.

❷ Laugh at the tempter.
Temptations are simply things that want to gain power over you. When you laugh at them, you reduce them to their proper place.

❸ Distract yourself with other, healthier activities.
God knows what's good for you and so do you. Find an alternate activity that promotes trust in God and requires you to care for your neighbors. Seek the company of others, especially people to whom you may be of service.

❹ Remember, your Lord also confronted temptation.
Jesus faced down temptation by telling the devil the truth, namely, only God is Lord. Consider using a contemporary version of Jesus' words: "God's in charge here, not you."

Even Jesus faced temptation when the devil confronted him in the wilderness.

❺ Tell the devil to go back to hell.
Consider saying this: "You're right, Mr. Devil. I'm a sinner. Unfortunately, you have no power here. My Lord loves sinners and has forgiven me forever. There's nothing you can do about it. Go back to where you came from and quit bothering me!"

Caution!

The following step should be reserved for the rare occasions when the above methods fail and should only be attempted under the counsel of authority.

❻ **Commit some minor sin to throw the devil off.**
Unchecked temptation often leads to apathy, confusion, and even despair, which is the archenemy of faith. To thwart this process, commit a minor sin to remind yourself that Jesus came specifically to save *you* from sin. Don't forget to include this sin in your later confession. (Luther sometimes advised people to do this—especially those in danger of despair.)

Be Aware

- There are different kinds of temptation. Regardless of the type, temptation always involves a hidden voice whispering to you, "Whatever God says, you really need to trust me instead. I'm the only thing that can help you."

- Temptations try to make us trust in ourselves or in other things more than in God. When you realize this, you'll see that everything on the list above is just turning back to Jesus who died to show you how much you can trust him.

HOW TO CARE FOR THE SICK

While a trained and licensed physician must be sought to treat illness and injury, there is no malady that cannot be helped with faithful attention and prayer.

1 Assess the nature of the problem.
Visit a local pharmacy if the illness is a simple one. Over-the-counter medications usually provide temporary relief until the body heals itself. If symptoms persist, the sick person should see a doctor and get a more detailed diagnosis.

2 Pray for them.
Intercessory prayers are prayers made on someone else's behalf. Recent studies point to healing in hospitalized patients who have been prayed for—even when the sick were not aware of the prayers. Add the afflicted person to your church's prayer list.

3 Call in the elders.
Prayer and emotional support from friends and family are vital parts of healing, living with illness, and facing death. Ask the pastor to assemble the church elders (leaders) for prayer and the laying on of hands.

Here's what the Bible says on this topic: "Are any among you sick? They should call for the elders of the church and have them pray over them, anointing them with oil in the name of the Lord" (James 5:14).

Be Aware

- Many people claim expertise in healing, from acupuncturists and herbalists to "faith healers" and psychics. Use caution and skepticism, but keep an open mind.

- Many people believe that much healing can be found in "comfort foods," such as homemade chicken soup.

- Those who attempt to diagnose and treat their own symptoms can often do more harm than good. When in doubt, always consult a pharmacist, doctor, or other medical professional.

Gather friends, family, and church leaders to pray and lay hands on sick people.

HOW TO IDENTIFY AND AVOID EVIL

The devil delights in unnoticed evil. To this end, the devil employs a wide array of lies, disguises, and deceptions while attacking our relationships with God and each other. A sharp eye and vigilance are your best defense. Lutherans dislike the subject of evil, but many secretly cultivate extraordinary talent for rooting it out.

❶ Know your enemy.
Evil appears in many forms, most often using camouflage to present itself as kindly or friendly. Cruelty, hatred, violence, and exploitation are among the many forms evil can take, but it often masquerades as justice or something done "for their own good." Be alert to acts, people, and events that employ these methods, even if the eventual outcome appears good.

❷ Proceed carefully and deliberately.
Avoid rushing to conclusions. Use good judgment.

❸ Take action to expose the evil.
Evil relies on darkness. It wants to remain hidden and hates the light of truth. Things that suffer from public knowledge or scrutiny might be evil.

❹ Be prepared to make a personal sacrifice.
Fighting evil can be costly. A successful counterattack may require you to give up something you cherish. For Jesus, as for many of his followers, it was his life. Love is the foundation of sacrifice that combats evil.

❺ Stay vigilant.

Evil's genius is shown in disguise, deception, and misdirection. Maintain your objectivity and apply the biblical measures of right and wrong you know to be correct. Martin Luther's standard was a conscience informed by Scripture and good common sense.

HOW TO AVOID GOSSIP

Gossip is among the most corrosive forces within a community and should be monitored closely. Discovery of gossip should be viewed as an opportunity to defend your neighbors' integrity, both gossiper and gossipee.

1 **Determine whether the conversation at hand qualifies as gossip.**

- Gossip involves one party speaking about a second party to a third party.

- The person who is the topic of gossip is not a participant in the conversation.

- The tone of the conversation is often secretive or negative. Gasps and whispers are common.

- The facts expressed in a gossip conversation are often unsubstantiated and have been obtained second- or third-hand.

2 **Recall and heed Titus 3:2: "Speak evil of no one."**

3 **Interject yourself into the conversation politely.**
Ask whether the gossiper(s) have spoken directly to the person about whom they are talking. If not, politely ask why. This may give some indication why they are gossiping.

4 **Make a statement of fact.**
Gossip withers in the face of truth. Make an attempt to parse out what is truly known from conjecture and supposition. State aloud that gossip is disrespectful and unfair.

Avoid gossip. It undermines community and damages relationships.

❺ Offer an alternative explanation based on fact. Describe other situations that cast the gossipee in a favorable light. Always try to give people the benefit of the doubt.

Be Aware

- There is a fine line between helping and meddling. Pay close attention to your own motivations and the possible outcomes of your actions.

- Gossip injures both the gossiper and the person who is the subject of rumors.

- Consult the Eighth Commandment and its explanation in Martin Luther's Small Catechism on page 199.

- For further help, consult James 4:11.

HOW TO BLESS SOMEONE

Blessings through history have had many purposes, often involving the passing of wealth or property from one person or generation to another. A Christian blessing is a declaration of the gospel of Jesus Christ to a specific individual— an affirmation that another person is claimed and loved by almighty God. Blessings should be dispensed liberally and with abandon.

❶ Evaluate the need at hand.
People have different needs at different times. When you perceive a need in which a blessing appears appropriate, take time to discern.

❷ Use safe touch.
Human touch is an affirmation with profound physical effects. Healing and emotional release are common. Make sure you use touch that is non-threatening, respectful, and communicates the love of Christ.

❸ Choose an appropriate way to give the blessing.
- Position one or both hands on the person's head. Use a light touch, but one firm enough to let the person know that he or she is being blessed.

- Place one hand on the person's shoulder.

- Trace a cross on the person's forehead.

- Hold both of the person's hands in yours while making good eye contact.

❹ Make a declaration of freedom.

- Blessings are often most effective when the spoken word is employed. For example: "[insert name here], child of God, you have been sealed by the Holy Spirit and marked with the cross of Christ forever."

- Consider ad-libbing a verbal blessing that speaks directly to the situation.

- Whenever possible, include the words spoken at baptism: "In the name of the Father, and of the Son, and of the Holy Spirit."

Be Aware

- Indirect blessings are often appropriate. These include but are not limited to favors, prayers, kind words, consolation, a hot meal, shared laughter, and acceptance.

- Some cultures consider head-touching impolite or even rude, so always ask permission before making a blessing this way.

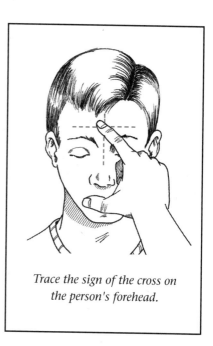

Trace the sign of the cross on the person's forehead.

HOW TO RESOLVE INTERPERSONAL CONFLICT

Disagreements are part of life. They often occur when we forget that not everyone sees things the same way. Conflict should be viewed as an opportunity to grow, not a contest for domination. Lutherans are traditionally shy, but when push comes to shove they value healthy relationships above all.

1 Adopt a healthy attitude.
Your frame of mind is critical. Approach the situation with forethought and calm. Prayer can be invaluable at this stage. Do not approach the other party when you're angry or upset.

2 Read Matthew 18:15-20 beforehand.
Consult the Bible to orient your thinking. This is the model Jesus provided and can be used to call to mind an appropriate method.

3 Talk directly to the person involved.
Avoid "triangulation." Talking about someone to a third party can make the conflict worse, as the person may feel that he or she is the subject of gossip. Speaking with the other person directly eliminates the danger and boosts the odds of a good outcome.

4 Express yourself without attacking.
Using "I statements" can avoid casting the other person as the "bad guy" and inflaming the conflict. "I statements" are sentences beginning with phrases such as "I feel ..." or "I'm uncomfortable when ..."

❺ Keep "speaking the truth in love" (Ephesians 4:15) as your goal.
Your "truth" may not be the other party's. Your objective is to discover and honor each other's "truth," not to put down the other person. Be ready to admit your own faults and mistakes.

❻ Seek out a third party to act as an impartial witness.
If direct conversation doesn't resolve the conflict, locate someone both parties trust to sit in. This can help clarify your positions and bring understanding.

❼ Build toward forgiveness and a renewed friendship.
Agree upon how you will communicate to prevent future misunderstandings.

Be Aware

- Seemingly unrelated events in your or the other person's life may be playing an invisible role in the conflict at hand. Be ready to shift the focus to the real cause.

- You may not be able to resolve the conflict at this time, but don't give up on future opportunities.

When two people aren't getting along, sometimes an impartial third person can help resolve the dispute.

HOW TO CONSOLE SOMEONE

Consolation is a gift from God. Christians in turn give it to others to build up the body of Christ and preserve it in times of trouble. (See 2 Corinthians 1:4-7.) Lutherans often employ food as a helpful secondary means.

❶ Listen first.
Make it known that you're present and available. When the person opens up, be quiet and attentive.

❷ Be ready to help the person face grief and sadness, not avoid them.
The object is to help the person name, understand, and work through his or her feelings, not gloss over them.

❸ Avoid saying things to make yourself feel better.
"I know exactly how you feel," is seldom true and trivializes the sufferer's pain. Even if you have experienced something similar, no experience is exactly the same. If there is nothing to say, simply be present with the person.

❹ Show respect with honesty.
Don't try to answer the mysteries of the universe or force your beliefs on the person. Be clear about the limitations of your abilities. Be ready to let some questions go unanswered. Consolation isn't about having all the answers, it's about bearing one another's burdens.

❺ Don't put words in God's mouth.
Avoid saying, "This is God's will," or, "This is part of God's plan." Unless you heard it straight from God, don't say it.

HOW TO COPE WITH LOSS AND GRIEF

Lutherans tend to downplay their losses by saying, "Well, it could be worse." This may provide only temporary relief at best. Any loss can cause pain, feelings of confusion, and uncertainty. These responses are normal.

1 Familiarize yourself with the stages of grief.
Experts identify five: denial, anger, bargaining, depression, and acceptance. Some add hope as a sixth stage. Grieving persons cycle back and forth through the stages, sometimes experiencing two or three in a single day. This is normal.

2 Express your grief.
Healthy ways may include crying, staring into space for extended periods, ruminating, shouting at the ceiling, and sudden napping. Laughing outbursts are also appropriate and should not be judged harshly.

3 Identify someone you trust to talk to.
Available people can include a spouse, parents, relatives, friends, a pastor, a doctor, or a trained counselor. Many household pets also make good listeners and willing confidants.

4 Choose a personal way to memorialize the loss.
Make a collage of photographs, offer a memorial donation to your church, or start a scrapbook of memories to honor the event. This helps you to begin to heal without getting stuck in your grief.

Be Aware

- Many experts prescribe a self-giving activity, such as volunteering at a shelter or soup kitchen, as a means of facilitating a healthy grieving process.

- The pain immediately after suffering a loss is usually deep and intense. This will lessen with the passage of time.

- Anger, guilt, bitterness, and sadness are likely emotions.

- Short-term depression may occur in extreme cases. After experiencing a great loss, such as the death of a loved one, make an appointment with your family physician for a physical.

- Even Jesus cried when his friend Lazarus died (John 11:35).

Even Jesus felt the loss of Lazarus when he died.

Mary   Martha

THE TOP 10 ATTRIBUTES TO LOOK FOR IN A SPOUSE

While no single personality trait can predict a compatible marriage, the following list frames the basic things to look for in a spouse. With all attributes, some differences can be the source of a couple's strength rather than a source of difficulty. Statistically, Lutherans appear to be about as successful at choosing a spouse as other people.

❶ Similar values.
Values that concern religious beliefs, life purpose, financial priorities, and children are a foundation on which to build the relationship. Contrary values tend to create discord.

❷ Physical-energy and physical-space compatibility.
Consider whether the person's energy level and physical-space needs work with yours. Also, the word *compatibility* can mean a complementary match of opposites, or it can denote a match based on strong similarities.

❸ Physical and romantic compatibility.
If the two of you have a similar degree of interest in or need for physical and romantic expression in your relationship, the chance of lifelong compatibility increases.

❹ Intellectual parity.
Communicating with someone who has a significantly different intelligence level or educational background can require extra effort.

⑤ Emotional maturity.
A lifelong relationship of mutual challenge and support often helps each person grow emotionally, but a lifetime spent waiting for someone to grow up could be more frustration than it's worth.

⑥ Sense of humor.
Sense of humor can provide an excellent measure of a person's personality and an important means to couple survival. If he or she doesn't get your jokes, you could be asking for trouble.

⑦ Respect.
Look for someone who listens to you without trying to control you. Look also for a healthy sense of self-respect.

⑧ Trustworthiness.
Seek out someone who is honest and acts with your best interests in mind—not only his or hers—and tries to learn from his or her mistakes.

⑨ Forgiving.
When you sincerely apologize to your spouse, he or she should try to work through and get beyond the problem rather than hold on to it. Once forgiven, past mistakes should not be raised, especially in conflict situations.

⑩ Kindness.
An attitude of consistent kindness may be the most critical attribute for a lifelong partnership.

Be Aware

- If you live to be old, you will probably experience major changes that you cannot predict at age 15 or 25 or 35. Accepting this fact in advance can help you weather difficult times.

- Use all of your resources—intuition, emotions, and rational thought—to make the decision about a life partner.

- Family members and trusted friends can offer invaluable advice in this decision-making process and should be consulted.

HOW TO BANISH THE DEVIL FROM YOUR PRESENCE

Since God loved the flesh so much as to redeem it by becoming flesh, Martin Luther believed that the devil, by contrast, hated the flesh. Bodily acts, therefore, hold the power to send the devil packing. While the existence of a "personal" devil—a physical entity embodying pure evil—is part of the Christian tradition, Lutherans tend to withhold final judgment on specifics. Still, it's good to be prepared.

❶ Laugh out loud.
Laughter is abhorrent to the devil and should be indulged in frequently.

❷ Make the sign of the cross.
The devil hates the cross because that is where God's love for you is most evident.

❸ Seek the company of other believers.
Play games with children, attend worship, join a prayer team, host a dinner party, or locate a Bible study. Solitude can provide the devil an opportunity.

❹ Serve those who have less than you.
Resolve to volunteer your time to help those less fortunate than you. The devil is thwarted by the love of Christ in action.

❺ Confess your sins.
The devil is attracted to a guilty conscience. Confession clears the conscience and emboldens the believer.

6 Break wind.
The devil (along with anyone else in the room) might well leave you alone. (This was one of Martin Luther's favorites.)

7 Consider what you might be doing to invite the devil into your life.
We invite the devil into our lives when our actions and values no longer center on Christ.

Banish the devil by taking part in activities with others.
Avoid excessive solitude.

HOW TO BE SAVED (BY GRACE THROUGH FAITH AND NOT BY YOUR GOOD WORKS)

Many religions are built on the idea that the more closely people follow the religious rules or the more morally people behave, the better God will like them—and the better God likes them, the greater their chances of "getting into heaven."

While there is nothing wrong with moral living or obeying God's laws, that kind of behavior has very little to do with the salvation God offers. You don't need to be a follower of Jesus Christ for that.

Christianity, on the other hand, says that out of pure love God was willing to sacrifice everything—even his only Son—to save you forever from sin, death, and all your false gods. Including you.

Since God has already done everything needed to secure your salvation through Jesus, you never have to do one single thing to earn God's favor, no matter how bad you are at following the rules. Still, being saved takes some getting used to.

❶ Get familiar with the word "grace."
Grace means that God gives you all the good stuff—forgiveness, salvation, love, and life, with all its ups and downs—as totally free gifts. Keep an eye out for situations in which you can use this word, and then use it liberally. You'll soon begin to see God's grace all around you.

❷ Practice letting go of things you love.
Staying focused on yourself can make it difficult to open up to a grace-filled world. But giving of yourself, your time, and your possessions can put you in a receptive, open frame of mind. This is important, as salvation cannot be "found" by looking for it, it is only revealed.

❸ Lose yourself as often as possible.
An important part of having a receptive frame of mind is losing yourself in whatever you're doing. To do this, give yourself over entirely to the activity. This can be accomplished in prayer and worship, but also through things like playing games, talking with friends and family, reading a good book, serving others, or playing a musical instrument. Even work can accomplish this.

❹ Admit your limitations.
Without straying into despair or false modesty, make an honest confession to yourself about what you can and cannot do, what you are and what you are not. When you see yourself realistically you become more open to God's message of love, grace, and salvation.

❺ Accept your uniqueness.
In God's eyes, you were so valuable as to merit the ultimate sacrifice of his Son, even before you spoke your first words. God will spend your whole life trying to convince you of this. When you accept that to God you are priceless beyond imagining it becomes easier to understand why God chose to save you.

❻ Spend time in worship and prayer to the living God.
While only God grants the faith that saves, the church gives lots of opportunities where God has promised to come to you.

7 Avoid the temptation to "do."

The "old Adam" or "old Eve" in you—the sinner in you—always wants to be in charge over God. He or she will tell you that God's grace is too good to be true and that you must "do" something to earn or justify it. Simply remind him or her that you were baptized into Jesus Christ and have all the grace you need.

Be Aware

- The apostle Paul's summary of the Gospel goes like this: "For by grace you have been saved through faith, and this is not your own doing; it is the gift of God—not the result of works, so that no one may boast" (Ephesians 2:8-9).

- This viewpoint about God's grace, even among many Christians, is unpopular, as it was when Martin Luther and the reformers reminded the church of it almost 500 years ago. Be aware that once you adopt it you will come under fire and be tempted to lapse back into the old way.

GRACE

Getting familiar with this very important word will help you get used to being saved.

HOW TO REFORM THE CHURCH WHEN IT STRAYS FROM THE GOSPEL

When Martin Luther nailed his Ninety-five Theses to the church door in 1517, he took a stand against the corruption he saw in the church—false gospels, immoral leaders, and bad theology—and launched the Reformation.

From then on, by hanging on to his belief that only the free gift of faith in Christ could save him—and that the institutional church could not—Luther took a stand for an idea that survives today: *Ecclesia semper reformanda est.* (This means, "The church must always reform.")

To stay faithful to the gospel, the church still depends on all its members to call it back, not to their own personal visions, but to Jesus' vision.

❶ Know your stuff.
You can't call the church back to the gospel if you don't learn for yourself what the gospel is. Read your Bible regularly. Also, spend time in conversation with good theologians, like pastors and church elders.

❷ Trust your conscience, but equip it first with good information.
To defy corrupt church authorities, Luther had to draw strength from even more powerful sources, namely his faith in God and his conscience. "It is neither safe nor right," he said, "to go against conscience."

❸ Double-check and triple-check your motivations. Are you fighting on behalf of the gospel or for your own personal agenda?
Knowing the difference between the two matters. Some things may be worthy social causes that deserve your time and attention, but they may not be the gospel.

❹ Speak out. Act.
It isn't enough just to take a stand or hold an opinion. Once you're sure you're doing it for the right reasons, find an effective way to make change happen.

Luther nailed the Ninety-five Theses in a public place (a common way to speak to the public in his day) and later used the printing press to spread his opinions to the widest possible audience. He put himself in the line of fire.

❺ Prepare to defend yourself, and your message of reform, from attack.
People tend to dislike reform—and institutions like it even less. While the church calls us to model the love of Christ and live by his teachings, sometimes the church and its leaders respond to reformers with a "kill the messenger" attitude.

❻ Keep steady, be patient, and listen to wise counsel.
The Reformation took decades to take root. During that time, Luther and other reformers battled church authorities. They also debated with each other about the best way to bring the gospel to a new age and restore the church to its real purpose.

Be Aware

- Not all efforts at reforming the church succeed. Refer to "How to Avoid Getting Burned at the Stake" on page 64 for more information.

How to Tell a Sinner from a Saint

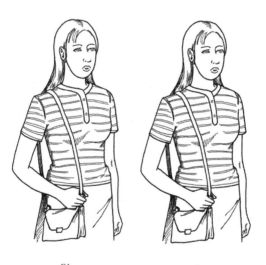

Sinner   Saint

It's impossible to tell a sinner from a saint, because all people are fully both. The church is filled with them.

HOW TO ENCOUNTER THE HOLY TRINITY AS ONE GOD IN THREE PERSONS

The Trinity is a mystery. Even great theologians don't completely understand, and some scholars spend their whole lives studying it. After 2,000 years, Christians still believe in this mystery because it gives life and shape to everything in our lives—our relationships, our faith, and especially our worship.

❶ Get to know the three Trinitarian creeds: the Nicene Creed, the Athanasian Creed, and the Apostles' Creed. Consider memorizing each one (two of them are pretty long).

These three "symbols," as they are sometimes called, were written during different times of crisis when heresies threatened the church's unity and clear statements about what Christians believed were needed. While different from each other, they each teach a lot about the three-personed God.

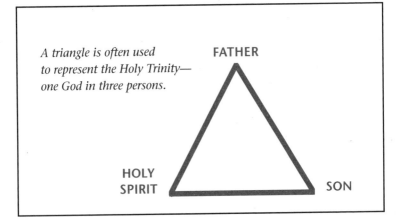

A triangle is often used to represent the Holy Trinity— one God in three persons.

FATHER

HOLY SPIRIT

SON

❷ Include the sign of the cross and the baptismal words as a regular part of your prayer life and worship life. The sign of the cross goes with the words, "In the name of the Father, and of the Son, and of the Holy Spirit," which traces a physical reminder of the Trinity on your body. For more information on making the sign of the cross, refer to the diagram on page 104.

❸ Understand that you were made in God's image. Just as the one God is Father, Son, and Holy Spirit all at once, you are mind, body, and soul all at once. Because you reflect the image of God you were made to live a life of worship in which everything you do and say honors God.

❹ Spend time in the community of faith. Go to worship, fellowship, Bible study, Sunday school, and anything else that regularly keeps you in the company of other Christians.

❺ Seek out God's Word and the means of grace. The Trinity is revealed in reading the Bible, preaching, the Sacraments, the forgiveness of sins, the community of believers, and within anything else where Jesus, the living Word, is active.

Be Aware

- Some people use handy metaphors to begin to get a handle on the doctrine of the Trinity. For example, water takes three major forms: liquid, solid, and gas. Yet it remains one substance. Such metaphors are very useful to a point, but ultimately they must give way to the divine mystery that remains.

HOW TO BECOME A THEOLOGIAN OF THE CROSS (AND AVOID BEING A THEOLOGIAN OF GLORY)

The term *theologian* technically means a student of or specialist in theology. And *theology* is the study of God and God's relationship with humanity and the universe. You may not consider yourself a specialist yet, but you definitely are a student of theology. To do this well, you may wish to follow in the footsteps of Martin Luther, who brought the Christian church away from a misguided "theology of glory" and back to the "theology of the cross."

❶ Position the cross in your thinking as an end point, not a starting point.
The cross of Jesus Christ is the most important and powerful thing in Christian faith. But it's easy to misunderstand what this means. A "theologian of glory," based on nothing more than individual wishes, tries to use the cross as a starting point for personal gain—to make people healthy and wealthy, successful and popular. A "theologian of the cross," in contrast, thinks of the cross as the last stop for sin, death, and delusions of grandeur. In other words, the cross is an end point.

❷ Determine to become a theologian of the cross.
The apostle Paul explains this approach: "For I decided to know nothing among you except Jesus Christ and him crucified" (1 Corinthians 2).

136   *The Lutheran Handbook*

❸ Identify the marks of the theology of glory and
practice contrasting them with the theology of
the cross.
A theologian of glory might say something like: "Accept
Jesus as your personal Lord and Savior and he will make
you happier, richer, and better looking." If things don't
pan out, the theologian of glory will say that you need
to have greater faith, believe more, or try harder.

A theologian of the cross, on the other hand, emphasizes
what Jesus did for us. In baptism, Jesus gives you his
word, which essentially says, "You are mine," even when
you feel troubled, poor, or unattractive.

❹ Look for God to reveal himself in the most
unexpected places.
A theologian of glory thinks that God shows up where
humans expect God to show up: in things that are powerful, wise, and important by human standards. On the
other hand, the theologian of the cross knows that God
is much subtler: God shows up in those things that
seem weak, foolish, and insignificant to human eyes.
(See 1 Corinthians 1:17-29.)

❺ Accept the lifelong nature of becoming a
theologian of the cross.
In the end, being a theologian of the cross is something
that can't be taught from a book. There's no class you
can take or diploma you can get that certifies you as
a theologian of the cross. As you experience life's ups
and downs, being a theologian of the cross is something
you just live into when you are open and trust God's
promises.

Everyday Stuff   137

BIBLE STUFF

Written down by many people over hundreds of years, the Bible is more like a portable bookshelf than one book by itself. And because the Bible is God's Word, people often feel overwhelmed when they try to read it.

This section includes:

- Helpful information about when, where, and why people wrote the 66 books within the Bible. (It didn't all come together at once.)

- Tips for reading and understanding the Bible— how it's organized and what it says.

- Some of the most mystifying, hair-raising, and just plain off-the-wall stories in the Bible.

COMMON TRANSLATIONS OF THE BIBLE

Translation	Grade Level*	Theological Affiliation	Year Released	Special Features
King James Version	12.0	Church of England, conservative and evangelical	1611	Poetic style using Elizabethan English. Most widely used translation for centuries.
New American Standard Bible	11.0	Conservative and evangelical	1971; updated, 1995	Revision of the 1901 American Standard Version into contemporary language.
New Revised Standard Version	8.1	Mainline and interconfessional	1989	Updated version of the Revised Standard Version.
New King James Version	8.0	Transnational, transdenominational, conservative, and evangelical	1982	Updates the King James text into contemporary language.
New International Version	7.8	Transnational, transdenominational, conservative, and evangelical	1978; revised, 1984	Popular modern-language version. Attempts to balance literal and dynamic translation methods.
Today's English Version (also called the	7.3	Evangelical and interconfessional	1976	Noted for its freshness of language.

Version	Grade level*	Theological perspective	Date	Description
New American Bible	6.6	Roman Catholic	1970; revised NT, 1986; revised Psalms, 1991	Official translation of the Roman Catholic Church in the United States.
New Living Translation	6.4	Evangelical	1996	A meaning-for-meaning translation. Successor to the Living Bible.
New Century Version	5.6	Conservative and evangelical	1988; revised, 1991	Follows the *Living Word Vocabulary*.
Contemporary English Version	5.4	Conservative, evangelical, mainline	1995	Easy-to-read English for new Bible readers.
The Message	4.8, from NT samples	Evangelical	2002	An expressive paraphrase of the Bible.

*The grade level on which the text is written, using Dale-chall, Fry, Raygor, and Spache Formulas.

Bible classifications

Apocrypha Bible: Contains certain books that Protestants don't consider canonical. Most of these OT books are accepted by the Roman Catholic Church.

Children's Bible: Includes illustrations and other study aids that are especially helpful for children.

Concordance Bible: Lists places in the Bible where key words are found.

Red Letter Bible: The words spoken by Christ appear in red.

Reference Bible: Pages include references to other Bible passages on the same subject.

Self-Proclaiming Bible: Diacritical marks (as in a dictionary) appear above difficult names and words to help with the pronunciation.

Text Bible: Contains text without footnotes or column references. May include maps, illustrations, and other helpful material.

60 ESSENTIAL BIBLE STORIES

	Story	Bible Text	Key Verse
1.	Creation	Genesis 1-2	Genesis 1:27
2.	The Human Condition	Genesis 3-4	Genesis 3:5
3.	The Flood and the First Covenant	Genesis 6-9	Genesis 9:8
4.	The Tower of Babel and Abraham and Sarah	Genesis 11-12	Genesis 12:1
5.	Sarah, Hagar, and Abraham	Genesis 12-25	Genesis 17:19
6.	Isaac and Rebecca	Genesis 22-25	Genesis 24:67
7.	Jacob and Esau	Genesis 25-36	Genesis 28:15
8.	Joseph and God's Hidden Ways	Genesis 37-50	Genesis 50:20
9.	Moses and Pharaoh	Exodus 1-15	Exodus 2:23
10.	The Ten Commandments	Exodus 20	Exodus 20:2
11.	From the Wilderness into the Promised Land	Exodus 16-18; Deuteronomy 1-6; Joshua 1-3, 24	Deuteronomy 6:4
12.	Judges	Book of Judges	Judges 21:25
13.	Ruth	Book of Ruth	Ruth 4:14
14.	Samuel and Saul	1 Samuel 1-11	1 Samuel 3:1
15.	King David	multiple OT books	1 Samuel 8:6
16.	David, Nathan, and What Is a Prophet?	2 Samuel 11-12	2 Samuel 7:12
17.	Solomon	1 Kings 1-11	1 Kings 6:12
18.	Split of the Kingdom	1 Kings 11ff	1 Kings 12:16
19.	Northern Kingdom, Its Prophets and Fate	1 Kings—2 Kings 17	Amos 5:21
20.	Southern Kingdom, Its Prophets and Fate (Part 1)	multiple OT books	Isaiah 5:7

60 ESSENTIAL BIBLE STORIES

	Story	Bible Text	Key Verse
21.	Southern Kingdom, Its Prophets and Fate (Part 2)	multiple OT books	Jeremiah 31:31
22.	The Exile	Isaiah 40-55; Ezekiel	Isaiah 40:10
23.	Return from Exile	multiple OT books	Ezra 1:1
24.	Ezra and Nehemiah	Books of Ezra and Nehemiah	Ezra 3:10
25.	Esther	Book of Esther	Esther 4:14
26.	Job	Book of Job	Job 1:1
27.	Daniel	Book of Daniel	Daniel 3:17
28.	Psalms of Praise and Trust	Psalms 8, 30, 100, 113, 121	Psalm 121:1
29.	Psalms for Help	various psalms	Psalm 22:1
30.	Wisdom	Job, Proverbs, Ecclesiastes	Proverbs 1:7
31.	The Annunciation	Luke 1:26-56	Luke 1:31-33
32.	Magi	Matthew 2:1-12	Matthew 2:2-3
33.	Birth of Jesus	Luke 2:1-20	Luke 2:10-11
34.	Simeon	Luke 2:25-35	Luke 2:30-32
35.	Wilderness Temptations	Matthew 4:1-11; Mark 1:12-13; Luke 4:1-13	Luke 4:12-13
36.	Jesus' Nazareth Sermon	Matthew 13:54-58; Mark 6:1-6: Luke 4:16-30	Luke 4:18-19, 21
37.	Jesus Calls the First Disciples	Matthew 4:18-22; Mark 1:16-20; Luke 5:1-11	Luke 5:9-10
38.	Beatitudes	Matthew 5:3-12	Luke 6:20-26
39.	Gerasene Demoniac	Matthew 8:28-34; Mark 5:1-20; Luke 8:26-39	Luke 8:39
40.	Feeding of the 5,000	Matthew 14:13-21; Mark 6:30-44; Luke 9:10-17; John 6:1-14	Luke 9:16-17

60 ESSENTIAL BIBLE STORIES

	Story	Bible Text	Key Verse
41.	The Transfiguration	Matthew 17:1-8; Mark 9:2-8: Luke 9:28-36	Luke 9:34-35
42.	Sending of the Seventy	Matthew 8:19-22; Luke 10:1-16	Luke 10:8, 16
43.	Good Samaritan	Luke 10:25-37	Luke 10:27-28
44.	Healing the Bent-Over Woman	Luke 13:10-17	Luke 13:16
45.	Parables of Lost and Found	Luke 15:1-32	Luke 15:31-32
46.	Rich Man and Lazarus	Luke 16:19-31	Luke 16:29-31
47.	Zacchaeus	Luke 19:1-11	Luke 19:9
48.	Sheep and Goats	Matthew 25:31-46	Matthew 25:40
49.	Parable of the Vineyard	Matthew 21:33-46; Mark 12:1-12; Luke 20:9-19; (Isaiah 5:1-7)	Luke 20:14-16
50.	The Last Supper	Matthew 26:20-29; Mark 14:12-16: Luke 22:14-38	Luke 22:19-20, 27
51.	Crucifixion	Matthew 27; Mark 15; Luke 23; John 19	Luke 23:42-43, 46
52.	Road to Emmaus	Luke 24	Luke 24:30-31
53.	Pentecost	Acts 2:1-21	Acts 2:17-18
54.	Healing the Lame Man	Acts 3-4	Acts 4:19
55.	Baptism of the Ethiopian	Acts 8:26-39	Acts 8:35-37
56.	Call of Saul	Acts 7:58—8:1, 9:1-30	Acts 9:15-16
57.	Peter and Cornelius	Acts 10	Acts 10:34-35
58.	Philippians Humility	Philippians 2:1-13	Philippians 2:12-13
59.	Love Hymn	1 Corinthians 13	1 Corinthians 13:4-7
60.	Resurrection	1 Corinthians 15	1 Corinthians 15:51-55

HOW TO READ THE BIBLE

The Bible is a collection of 66 separate books gathered together over hundreds of years and thousands of miles. Divided into the Old Testament (Hebrew language) and the New Testament (Greek language), these writings have many authors and take many forms.

The Bible includes histories, stories, prophecies, poetry, songs, teachings, and laws, to name a few. Christians believe the Bible is the story of God's relationship with humankind and a powerful way that God speaks to people.

❶ Determine your purpose for reading.
Clarify in your own mind what you hope to gain. Your motivations should be well intentioned, such as to seek information, to gain a deeper understanding of God and yourself, or to enrich your faith. Pray for insight before every reading time.

❷ Resolve to read daily.
Commit to a daily regimen of Bible reading. Make it a part of your routine until it becomes an unbreakable habit.

Commit to reading the Bible daily.

❸ Master the mechanics.
- Memorize the books of the Bible in order.

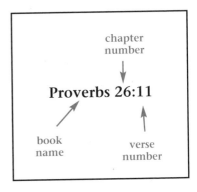

chapter
number

Proverbs 26:11

book
name

verse
number

- Familiarize yourself with the introductory material. Many Bible translations include helpful information at the front of the Bible and at the beginning of each book.

- The books are broken down into chapters and verses. Locate the beginning of a book by using the Bible's table of contents. Follow the numerical chapter numbers; these are usually in large type. Verses are likewise numbered in order within each chapter. Simply run your finger down the page until you locate the verse number you're looking for.

- If your Bible contains maps (usually in the back), consult them when cities, mountains, or seas are mentioned in your reading.

❹ Befriend the written text.
Read with a pen or pencil in hand and underline passages of interest. Look up unfamiliar words in a dictionary. Write notes in the margins when necessary. The Bible was written to be read and used, not worshiped.

❺ Practice reading from the Bible out loud.

HOW TO MEMORIZE A BIBLE VERSE

Memorizing Scripture is an ancient faith practice. Its value is often mentioned by people who have, in crisis situations, remembered comforting or reassuring passages coming to mind, sometimes decades after first memorizing them. There are three common methods of memorization.

Method 1: Memorize with Music

Choose a verse that is special for you. It is more difficult to remember something that doesn't make sense to you or that lacks meaning.

❶ Choose a familiar tune.
Pick something catchy and repetitious.

❷ Add the words from the Bible verse to your tune.
Mix up the words a bit, if necessary. Memorizing a verse "word for word" isn't always as important as learning the message of the verse.

❸ Mark the verse in your Bible.
This will help you find it again later on. Consider highlighting or underlining it.

❹ Make the words rhyme, if possible.

Method 2: The Three S's
(See it, Say it, Script it)

This method works on the principle of multisensory reinforcement. The brain creates many more neural pathways to a memory through sight, speech, and manipulation (writing) than just one of these, so recall is quicker and easier.

❶ Write the verse on index cards in large print. Post the cards in places you regularly look, such as the refrigerator door or bathroom mirror.

❷ Say the verse out loud. Repeat the verse 10 times to yourself every time you notice one of your index cards.

❸ Write the verse down.

❹ Try saying and writing the verse at the same time. Repeat.

Write the verse out longhand several dozen times.

Method 3: Old-Fashioned Memorization

Attempt this method only if you consider yourself to be "old school" or if the other methods fail.

❶ Write the verse out by hand on paper.
A whiteboard can work extremely well, also. Consider writing it as many as 100 times. Repeat this process until you can recite the verse flawlessly.

❷ Don't get up until you've memorized the verse.
Open your Bible to the appropriate verse, sit down in front of it, and don't get up, eat, sleep, or use the bathroom until you can recite it flawlessly.

❸ Enlist a family member or friend to help you.
Have them read along with you and prompt you when you get stuck.

THE TOP 10 BIBLE VILLAINS

❶ Satan
The Evil One is known by many names in the Bible and appears many places, but the devil's purpose is always the same: To disrupt and confuse people so they turn from God and seek to become their own gods. This Bible villain is still active today.

❷ The Serpent
In Eden, the serpent succeeded in tempting Eve to eat from the tree of the knowledge of good and evil (Genesis 3:1-7). As a result, sin entered creation. If it weren't for the serpent, we'd all still be walking around naked, eating fresh fruit, and living forever.

❸ Pharaoh (probably Seti I or Rameses II)
The notorious Pharaoh from the book of Exodus enslaved the Israelites. Moses eventually begged him to "Let my people go," but Pharaoh hardened his heart and refused. Ten nasty plagues later, Pharaoh relented, but then changed his mind again. In the end, with his army at the bottom of the sea, Pharaoh finally gave his slaves up to the wilderness.

❹ Goliath
"The Philistine of Gath," who stood six cubits in height (about nine feet tall), was sent to fight David, still a downy-headed youth of 15. Goliath was a fighting champion known for killing people, but David drilled Goliath in the head with a rock from his sling and gave God the glory (1 Samuel 17).

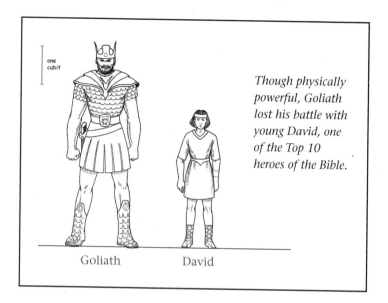

one
cubit

Though physically powerful, Goliath lost his battle with young David, one of the Top 10 heroes of the Bible.

Goliath   David

⑤ Jezebel

King Ahab of Judah's wife and a follower of the false god Baal, Jezebel led her husband away from God and tried to kill off the prophets of the Lord. Elijah the prophet, however, was on the scene. He shamed Jezebel's false prophets and killed them (1 Kings 18:40).

⑥ King Herod

Afraid of any potential threat to his power, upon hearing about the birth of the Messiah in Bethlehem Herod sent the Wise Men to pinpoint his location. Awestruck by the Savior in the cradle, the Wise Men went home by a different route and avoided Herod. In a rage, he ordered the murder of every child two years of age or younger in the vicinity of Bethlehem. The baby Messiah escaped with his parents to Egypt (Matthew 2:14-15).

❼ The Pharisees, Sadducees, and Scribes
They dogged Jesus throughout his ministry, alternately challenging his authority and being awed by his power. It was their leadership, with the consent and blessing of the people and the Roman government that brought Jesus to trial and execution.

❽ Judas
One of Jesus' original disciples, Judas earned 30 pieces of silver by betraying his Lord over to the authorities. He accomplished this by leading the soldiers into the garden of Gethsemane where he revealed Jesus with a kiss (Matthew 26–27).

❾ Pontius Pilate
The consummate politician, the Roman governor chose to preserve his own bloated status by giving the people what they wanted: Jesus' crucifixion. He washed his hands to signify self-absolution, but bloodied them instead.

❿ God's People
They whine, they sin, they turn their backs on God over and over again. When given freedom, they blow it. When preached repentance by God's prophets, they stone them. When offered a Savior, we kill him. In the end, it must be admitted, God's people—us!—don't really shine. Only by God's grace and the gift of faith in Jesus Christ do we have hope.

THE TOP 10 BIBLE HEROES

The Bible is filled with typical examples of heroism, but another kind of hero inhabits the pages of the Bible—those people who, against all odds, follow God no matter the outcome. These are heroes of faith.

❶ Noah

In the face of ridicule from others, Noah trusted God when God chose him to build an ark to save a remnant of humanity from destruction. Noah's trust became part of a covenant with God.

Noah trusted God, even though others made fun of him. By following God's instructions and building a great ark, Noah and his family survived the flood (Genesis 6–10).

❷ Abraham and Sarah

In extreme old age, Abraham and Sarah answered God's call to leave their home and travel to a strange land, where they became the parents of God's people.

❸ Moses

Moses, a man with a speech impediment, challenged the Egyptian powers to deliver God's people from bondage. He led a rebellious and contrary people for 40 years through the wilderness and gave them God's law.

❹ Rahab

A prostitute who helped Israel conquer the promised land, Rahab was the great-grandmother of King David, and thus a part of the family of Jesus himself.

❺ David

Great King David, the youngest and smallest member of his family, defeated great enemies, turning Israel into a world power. He wrote psalms, led armies, and confessed his sins to the Lord.

❻ Mary and Joseph

These humble peasants responded to God's call to be the parents of the Messiah, although the call came through a pregnancy that was not the result of marriage.

❼ The Canaanite Woman

Desperate for her daughter's health, the Canaanite woman challenged Jesus regarding women and race by claiming God's love for all people (Matthew 15:21-28). Because of this, Jesus praised her faith.

❽ Peter

Peter was a man quick to speak but slow to think. At Jesus' trial, Peter denied ever having known him. But in the power of forgiveness and through Christ's appointment, Peter became a leader in the early church.

❾ Saul/Paul

Originally an enemy and persecutor of Christians, Paul experienced a powerful vision of Jesus, converted, and became the greatest missionary the church has ever known.

❿ Phoebe

A contemporary of Paul's, Phoebe is believed to have delivered the book of Romans after traveling some 800 miles from Cenchrea near Corinth to Rome. A wealthy woman, she used her influence to travel, protect other believers, and to host worship services in her home.

Phoebe is believed to have delivered the book of Romans after traveling 800 miles.

THE THREE MOST REBELLIOUS THINGS JESUS DID

❶ The prophet returned to his hometown (Luke 4:14-27).
Jesus returned to Nazareth, where he was raised and was invited to read Scripture and preach. First, he insisted that the scriptures he read were not just comforting promises of a distant future, but that they were about him, local boy, anointed by God. Second, he insisted God would bless foreigners with those same promises through him. These statements amounted to the unpardonable crime of blasphemy!

❷ The rebel thumbed his nose at the authorities (John 11:55—12:11).
Jesus had become an outlaw, hunted by the religious authorities who wanted to kill him. Mary, Martha, and Lazarus threw a thank-you party for Jesus in Bethany, right outside Jerusalem, the authorities' stronghold. In spite of the threats to his life, Jesus went to the party. This was not just rebellion but a demonstration of how much Jesus loved his friends.

❸ The king rode a royal procession right under Caesar's nose (Matthew 21:1-17; Mark 11:1-10; Luke 19:28-38; John 12:12-19).
Jesus entered Jerusalem during a great festival, in full view of adoring crowds, as a king come home to rule. Riding the colt, heralded by the people with cloaks and branches, accompanied by the royal anthem (Psalm 118), he rode in to claim Jerusalem for God and himself as God's anointed. The Roman overlords and the Jewish leaders watched this seditious act and prepared for a crucifixion.

THE SEVEN FUNNIEST BIBLE STORIES

Humor isn't scarce in the Bible; you just have to look for it. For example, God tells Abraham (100 years old) and Sarah (in her 90s) they'll soon have a son. Understandably, they laugh. Later, they have a son named Isaac, which means "he laughs." Bible humor is also ironic, gross, and sometimes just plain bizarre.

❶ Gideon's dog-men (Judges 6:11—7:23).
God chooses Gideon to lead an army against the Midianites. Gideon gathers an army of 32,000 men, but this is too many. God tells Gideon to make all the men drink from a stream, and then selects only the 300 men who lap water like dogs.

❷ David ambushes Saul in a cave while he's "busy" (1 Samuel 24:2-7).
While pursuing David cross-country to engage him in battle, Saul goes into a cave to "relieve himself" (move his bowels). Unbeknownst to Saul, David and his men are already hiding in the very same cave. While Saul's doing his business, David sneaks up and cuts off a corner of Saul's cloak with a knife. Outside afterward, David shows King Saul the piece of cloth to prove he could have killed him "on the throne."

❸ King David does the goofy (2 Samuel 12-23).
David is so excited about bringing the Ark of the Covenant to Jerusalem that he dances before God and all the people dressed only in a linen ephod, an apron-like garment that covered only the front of his body.

The doomed city of Sodom

Lot's wife ignored God's warning. She looked back at the city of Sodom and became a pillar of salt.

Pillar of salt (formerly Lot's wife)

❹ **Lot's wife (Genesis 19:24-26).**
While fleeing God's wrath upon the cities of Sodom and Gomorrah, Lot's wife forgets (or ignores) God's warning not to look back upon the destruction and turns into a woman-sized pillar of salt.

❺ **Gerasene demoniac (Mark 5:1-20).**
A man is possessed by so many demons that chains cannot hold him. Jesus exorcises the demons and sends them into a herd of 2,000 pigs, which then run over the edge of a cliff and drown in the sea. The herders, now 2,000 pigs poorer, get miffed and ask Jesus to leave.

6 Disciples and loaves of bread (Mark 8:14-21).
The disciples were there when Jesus fed 5,000 people
with just five loaves of bread and two fish. They also
saw him feed 4,000 people with seven loaves. Later, in a
boat, the disciples fret to an exasperated Jesus because
they have only one loaf for 13 people.

7 Peter can't swim (Matthew 14:22-33).
Blundering Peter sees Jesus walking on the water and
wants to join him. But when the wind picks up,
Peter panics and starts to sink. In Greek, the name
Peter means "rock."

*Peter, "the rock,"
sank when he looked
to himself instead of
to Jesus. Jesus later
described Peter as a
Rock of the church
(Matthew 16:18).*

THE FIVE GROSSEST BIBLE STORIES

1 Eglon and Ehud (Judges 3:12-30).
Before kings reigned over Israel, judges ruled the people. At that time, a very overweight king named Eglon conquered Israel and demanded money. A man named Ehud brought the payment to Eglon while he was perched on his "throne" (meaning "toilet"). Along with the money, Ehud handed over a little something extra—his sword, which he buried so far in Eglon's belly that the sword disappeared into the king's fat and, as the Bible says, "the dirt came out" (v. 22).

2 Job's sores (Job 2:1-10).
Job lived a righteous life yet he suffered anyway. He had oozing sores from the bald spot on top of his head clear down to the soft spot on the bottom of his foot. Job used a broken piece of pottery to scrape away the pus that leaked from his sores.

3 The naked prophet (Isaiah 20).
God's prophets went to great lengths to get God's message across to the people. Isaiah was no exception. God's people planned a war, but God gave it the thumbs down. Isaiah marched around Jerusalem naked *for three years* as a sign of what would happen if the people went to war.

Jeremiah strapped on some filthy underwear to show God could no longer be proud of the people.

Filthy
underwear

❹ **The almost-naked prophet (Jeremiah 13:1-11).**
God sent Jeremiah to announce that God could no longer be proud of the people. To make the point, Jeremiah bought a new pair of underclothes, wore them every day without washing them, then buried them in the wet river sand. Later, he dug them up, strapped them on, and shouted that this is what has happened to the people who were God's pride!

❺ **Spilling your guts (Matthew 27:1-8; Acts 1:16-19).**
Judas betrayed Jesus and sold him out for 30 pieces of silver. He bought a field with the ill-gotten loot. Guilt-stricken, Judas walked out to the field, his belly swelled up until it burst, and his intestines spilled out on to the ground.

FIVE FACTS ABOUT LIFE IN OLD TESTAMENT TIMES

❶ Almost everyone wore sandals.
They were called "sandals" because people walked on sand much of the time.

❷ There were no newspapers.
People got news by hearing it from other people. Spreading important news was like a giant game of "telephone."

❸ It was dark.
Homes, often tents, were typically lit at night by an oil lamp, if at all.

❹ You had to fetch your water, which was scarce.
Rich folks had servants to carry it for them, but most people had to carry household water in jugs or leather bags, usually some distance, from a river or well.

❺ Life expectancy was short.
Despite some long-lived exceptions described in the book of Genesis, such as Abraham (175 years) and Methuselah (969 years), few people lived past 50.

Sandals were made for walking on sand.

TEN IMPORTANT THINGS THAT HAPPENED BETWEEN THE OLD AND NEW TESTAMENTS

The period of time described in the Old Testament ended about 400 years before Jesus' birth. The people of God kept living, believing, struggling, and writing during that period. Here are some of the important events that took place between the Testaments.

❶ The Hebrew nation dissolved.
In 587 B.C., the Babylonians destroyed Jerusalem and Solomon's temple, and took the people into exile. Judah was never again an independent kingdom.

❷ The people scattered.
After the exile to Babylon ended, the people of Judah moved to many different places. Some of them later came back, but many never did. Some of them lived in Babylon, some lived in Egypt, and some just scattered elsewhere.

❸ A religion replaced a nation.
As a result of items 1 and 2, the people's religion changed. They no longer had a state or national religion (Judean religion). Instead, they had a freestanding faith called Judaism.

4 The Aramaic language became popular.
Because Aramaic was the international language of the Persian Empire, many Jews quit speaking Hebrew and spoke Aramaic instead. This is why Jesus spoke Aramaic.

5 Alexander the Great conquered the world.
Around 330 B.C., Alexander the Great conquered the Mediterranean and Mesopotamian world. As a result, Greek became the everyday language of business and trade in the region. This is why the New Testament was written in Greek.

6 The hammer dropped.
Around 170 B.C., the Seleucid emperor outlawed circumcision and the Sabbath, and defiled the temple. A family of Jews called the Maccabees (which means "hammer") led a revolt.

7 The Hebrew Scriptures were finished.
During this time, the individual books that make up what we call the Old Testament were finished. Several other religious books written at this time (mostly in Greek) aren't in the Protestant Bible but are part of the Apocrypha.

8 The Sadducees, Pharisees, Essenes, Samaritans, Zealots, and other groups of people sprouted up.
Different schools of thought developed within Judaism. Most of their disagreements were over the idea that God's people would be resurrected to eternal life.

❾ God seemed to have forgotten the promise.

God promised King David that one of his descendants would always be king in Jerusalem. But after the Babylonian exile, there were no kings in Jerusalem. People wondered what had happened to God's promise.

❿ The Roman Empire expanded.

In 63 B.C., the Roman Empire conquered Palestine, having already conquered pretty much everyone else in the region. This is why the Roman Empire ruled the area during the time of Jesus and the New Testament.

FIVE FACTS ABOUT LIFE IN NEW TESTAMENT TIMES

❶ Synagogues were not always buildings.
For worship, Jesus' people gathered in all kinds of places, often outdoors. "Church" was any gathering of people for worship.

❷ Houses were boxy.
Most houses had a flat roof with an outside staircase leading to it. Inhabitants would sleep on the roof during hot weather.

Houses in New Testament times were boxy.

❸ Every town had a marketplace.
Usually there was just one marketplace per town, but one could buy almost everything needed to live.

❹ People ate a lot of fish.
The most common fish in the Sea of Galilee were catfish and carp. Roasting over a charcoal fire was the most common method of cooking.

❺ Dogs were shunned.
The Jewish people in Jesus' day did not keep dogs as pets. Dogs were considered unclean because they ate garbage and animal carcasses.

THE FIVE BIGGEST MISCONCEPTIONS ABOUT THE BIBLE

1 **The Bible was written in a short period of time.**
Christians believe that God inspired the Bible writers, the first of whom may have been Moses. God inspired people to write down important histories, traditions, songs, wise sayings, poetry, and prophetic words. All told—from the first recordings of the stories in Genesis to the last decisions about Revelation—the entire Bible formed over a period spanning anywhere from 800 to 1,400 years!

2 **One person wrote the Bible.**
Unlike Islam's Koran, which was written by the prophet Muhammad, the books of the Bible claim the handiwork of many people. Much of Scripture does not identify the human hand that wrote it, so some parts of the Bible may have been written by women as well as men.

3 **The entire Bible should be taken literally.**
While many parts of the Bible are meant as descriptions of actual historical events, other parts are intended as *illustrations of God's truth*, such as Song of Solomon, the book of Revelation, and Jesus' parable of the good Samaritan. So when Jesus says, "If your right eye causes you to sin, tear it out and throw it away" (Matthew 5:29), please do not take the saying literally!

❹ People in Bible times were unenlightened.
During the 1,400 years it took to write the Bible, some of history's greatest thinkers lived and worked. Many of these philosophers, architects, mathematicians, orators, theologians, historians, doctors, military tacticians, inventors, engineers, poets, and playwrights are still quoted today and their works are still in use.

❺ The Bible is a single book.
The Bible is actually a collection of books, letters, and other writings—more like a library than a book. There are 39 books in the Hebrew scriptures, what Christians call the "Old" Testament, and 27 books (mostly letters) in the New Testament. There are seven books in the Apocryhpha (books written between the Old and New Testaments), or "deuterocanonical" books.

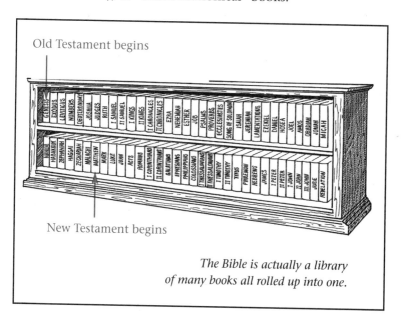

The Bible is actually a library of many books all rolled up into one.

JESUS' TWELVE APOSTLES (PLUS JUDAS AND PAUL)

While Jesus had many disciples (students and followers) the Bible focuses particularly on twelve who were closest to him. Tradition says that these twelve spread Jesus' message throughout the known world (Matthew 28:18-20). For this reason, they were known as *apostles*, a word that means "sent ones."

❶ Andrew
A fisherman and the first disciple to follow Jesus, Andrew brought his brother, Simon Peter, to Jesus.

❷ Bartholomew
Also called Nathanael, tradition has it that he was martyred by being skinned alive.

❸ James the Elder
James, with John and Peter, was one of Jesus' closest disciples. Herod Agrippa killed James because of his faith, which made him a martyr (Acts 12:2).

❹ John
John (or one of his followers) is thought to be the author of the Gospel of John and three letters of John. He probably died of natural causes in old age.

❺ Matthew
Matthew was a tax collector and, therefore, probably an outcast even among his own people. He is attributed with the authorship of the Gospel of Matthew.

❻ Peter

Peter was a fisherman who was brought to faith by his brother Andrew. He was probably martyred in Rome by being crucified upside down.

❼ Philip

Philip, possibly a Greek, is responsible for bringing Bartholomew (Nathanael) to faith. He is thought to have died in a city called Phrygia.

❽ James the Less

James was called "the Less" so he wouldn't be confused with James, the brother of John, or James, Jesus' brother.

❾ Simon

Simon is often called "the Zealot." Zealots were a political group in Jesus' day that favored the overthrow of the Roman government by force.

❿ Jude

Jude may have worked with Simon the Zealot in Persia (Iran) where they were martyred on the same day.

⓫ Thomas

"Doubting" Thomas preached the message of Jesus in India.

⓬ Matthias

Matthias was chosen by lot to replace Judas. It is thought that he worked mostly in Ethiopia.

⓭ Judas Iscariot

Judas was the treasurer for Jesus' disciples and the one who betrayed Jesus for 30 pieces of silver. According to the Bible, Judas killed himself for his betrayal.

⓮ Paul

Paul is considered primarily responsible for bringing non-Jewish people to faith in Jesus. He traveled extensively and wrote many letters to believers. Many of Paul's letters are included in the New Testament.

THE FIVE WEIRDEST LAWS IN THE OLD TESTAMENT

The Old Testament has many helpful, common sense laws, such as "You shall not kill," and, "You shall not steal." But there are a few others that need some explaining.

❶ The "ox" law.

"When an ox gores a man or a woman to death, the ox shall be stoned, and its flesh shall not be eaten; but the owner of the ox shall not be liable" (Exodus 21:28). Replace "ox" with "car" and the law makes more sense—it is about protecting others from reckless actions.

People living in biblical times were sometimes gored by oxen.

People who were gored by oxen—or victims of other crimes—had legal recourse.

❷ The "no kid boiling" law.
"You shall not boil a kid in its mother's milk" (Exodus 23:19b). A "kid," of course, is a juvenile goat, not a human being.

❸ The "which bugs are legal to eat" law.
"All winged insects that walk upon all fours are detestable to you. But among the winged insects that walk on all fours you may eat those that have jointed legs above their feet" (Leviticus 11:20-21). The law is unclear whether it is legal to eat the bug if you first pull off the legs.

❹ The "don't eat blood" law.
"No person among you shall eat blood" (Leviticus 17:12). Some laws beg the question whether people in that time had any sense of taste.

❺ The "pure cloth" law.
"You shall not wear clothes made of wool and linen woven together" (Deuteronomy 22:11). Polyester came along after Bible times.

THE TOP 10 BIBLE MIRACLES AND WHAT THEY MEAN

❶ Creation.

God created the universe and everything that is in it, and God continues to create and recreate without ceasing. God's first and ongoing miracle was to reveal that the creation has a purpose.

❷ The Passover.

The Israelites were enslaved by Pharaoh, a ruler who believed the people belonged to him, not to God. In the last of 10 plagues, God visited the houses of all the Egyptians to kill the firstborn male in each one. God alone is Lord of the people, and no human can claim ultimate power over us.

❸ The Exodus.

God's people were fleeing Egypt when Pharaoh dispatched his army to force them back into slavery. The army trapped the people with their backs to a sea, but God parted the water and the people walked across to freedom while Pharaoh's minions were destroyed. God chose to free us from all forms of tyranny so we may use that freedom to serve God and each other.

❹ Manna.

After the people crossed the sea to freedom, they complained that they were going to starve to death. They even asked to go back to Egypt. God sent manna, a form of bread, so the people lived. God cares for us even when we give up, pine for our slavery, and lose faith. God never abandons us.

❺ The Incarnation.
The immortal and infinite God became a human being, choosing to be born of a woman. God loved us enough to become one of us in Jesus of Nazareth, forever bridging the divide that had separated us from God.

❻ Jesus healed the paralyzed man.
Some men brought a paralyzed friend to Jesus. Jesus said, "Son, your sins are forgiven" (Mark 2:5). This means that Jesus has the power to forgive our sins—and he does so as a free gift.

❼ Jesus calmed the storm.
Jesus was asleep in a boat with his disciples when a great storm came up and threatened to sink it. He said, "Peace! Be still!" (Mark 4:39). Then the storm immediately calmed. Jesus is Lord over even the powers of nature.

❽ The Resurrection.
Human beings executed Jesus, but God raised him from the dead on the third day. Through baptism, we share in Jesus' death, so we will also share in eternal life with God the Father, Son, and Holy Spirit. Christ conquered death.

❾ Pentecost.
Jesus ascended from the earth, but he did not leave the church powerless or alone. On the 50th day after the Jewish Passover (*Pentecost* means 50th), Jesus sent the Holy Spirit to create the church and take up residence among us. The Holy Spirit is present with us always.

❿ The Second Coming.
One day, Christ will come again and end all suffering. This means that the final result of the epic battle between good and evil is already assured. It is simply that evil has not yet admitted defeat.

THE EXODUS

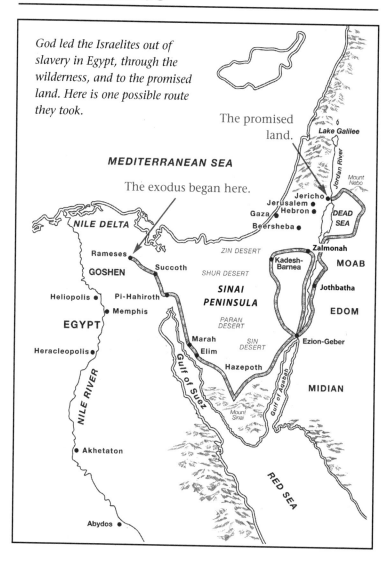

God led the Israelites out of slavery in Egypt, through the wilderness, and to the promised land. Here is one possible route they took.

The promised land.

Lake Galilee

Jordan River

Mount Nebo

MEDITERRANEAN SEA

The exodus began here.

NILE DELTA

Jerusalem
Jericho
Gaza Hebron
Beersheba

DEAD SEA

Rameses

Zalmonah

ZIN DESERT

GOSHEN
Succoth

SHUR DESERT

Kadesh-Barnea

MOAB

Heliopolis
Pi-Hahiroth
Memphis

SINAI PENINSULA

Jothbatha

EGYPT

PARAN DESERT

EDOM

Heracleopolis

Marah
Elim

SIN DESERT

Ezion-Geber

Hazepoth

MIDIAN

Gulf of Suez

Gulf of Aqabah

NILE RIVER

Mount Sinai

Akhetaton

RED SEA

Abydos

THE HOLY LAND—
OLD TESTAMENT TIMES

THE HOLY LAND—
NEW TESTAMENT TIMES

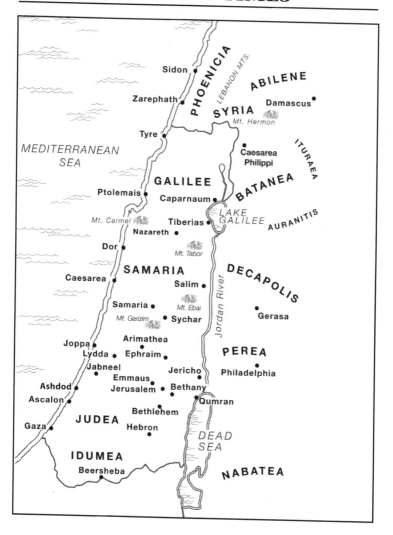

PAUL'S JOURNEYS

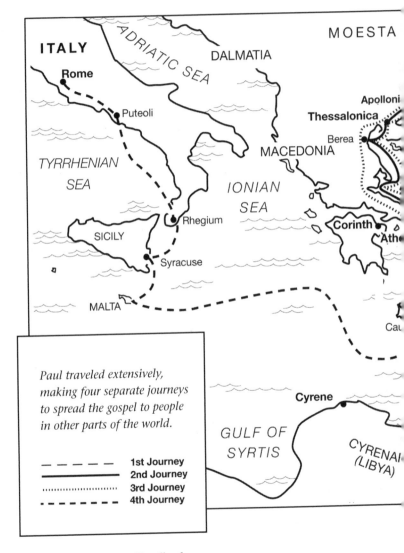

Paul traveled extensively, making four separate journeys to spread the gospel to people in other parts of the world.

– – – – –	1st Journey
——————	2nd Journey
....	3rd Journey
▪ – ▪ – ▪ – ▪	4th Journey

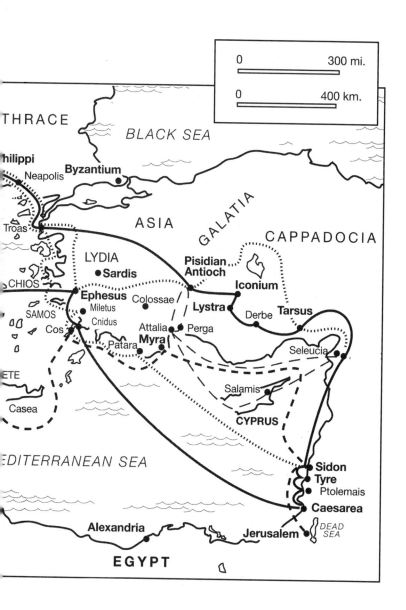

JERUSALEM IN JESUS' TIME

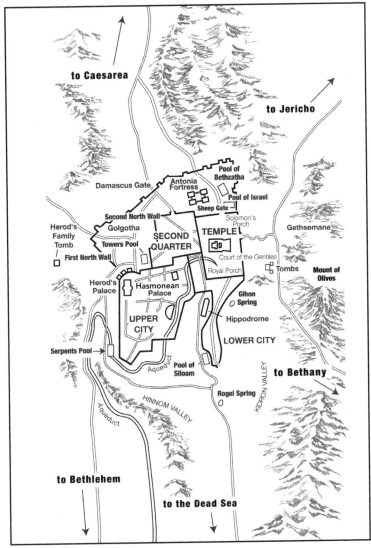

to Caesarea

to Jericho

Pool of Bethzatha

Antonia Fortress

Pool of Israel

Damascus Gate

Sheep Gate

Solomon's Porch

Gethsemane

Second North Wall

Golgotha

SECOND QUARTER

TEMPLE

Herod's Family Tomb

Towers Pool

Court of the Gentiles

First North Wall

Royal Porch

Tombs

Mount of Olives

Herod's Palace

Hasmonean Palace

Gihon Spring

UPPER CITY

Hippodrome

Serpents Pool

LOWER CITY

Aqueduct

Pool of Siloam

to Bethany

KIDRON VALLEY

HINNOM VALLEY

Rogel Spring

Aqueduct

to Bethlehem

to the Dead Sea

NOAH'S ARK

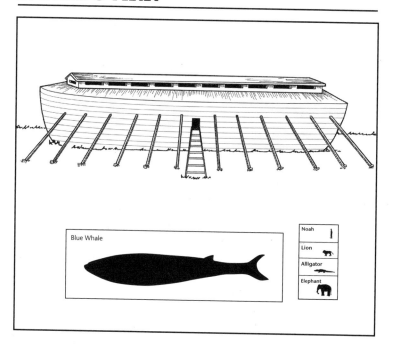

A cubit is equal to the length of a man's forearm from the elbow to the tip of the middle finger—approximately 18 inches or 45.7 centimeters. Noah's ark was 300 cubits long, 50 cubits wide, and 30 cubits tall (Genesis 6:15).

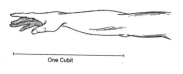

One Cubit

THE ARK OF THE COVENANT

God told the Israelites to place the stone tablets—the "covenant"—of the law into the Ark of the Covenant. The Israelites believed that God was invisibly enthroned above the vessel and went before them wherever they traveled.

The Ark of the Covenant was 2.5 cubits long and 1.5 cubits wide (Exodus 25:17).

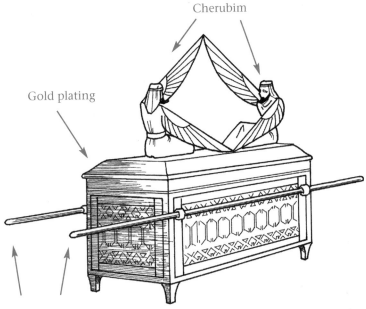

Cherubim

Gold plating

Carrying poles

Exodus 25:10-22

SOLOMON'S TEMPLE

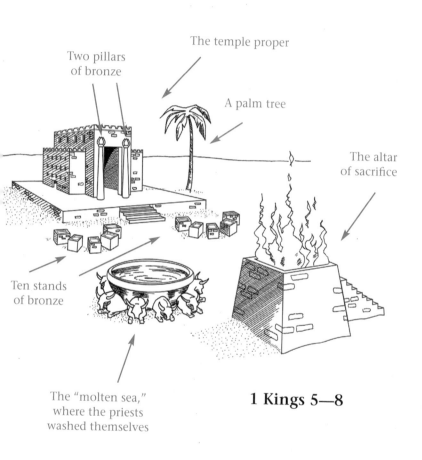

Two pillars of bronze

The temple proper

A palm tree

The altar of sacrifice

Ten stands of bronze

The "molten sea," where the priests washed themselves

1 Kings 5—8

THE ARMOR OF GOD

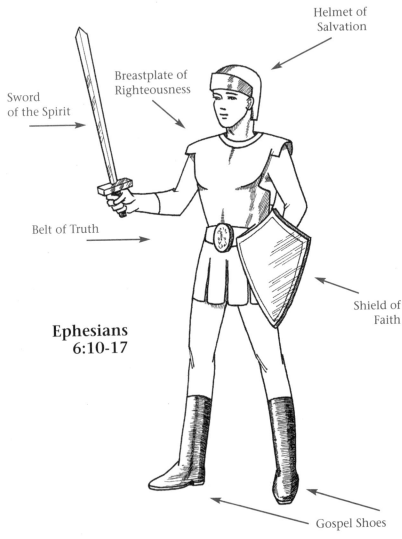

Helmet of
Salvation

Breastplate of
Righteousness

Sword
of the Spirit

Belt of Truth

Shield of
Faith

**Ephesians
6:10-17**

Gospel Shoes

THE PASSION AND CRUCIFIXION

Judas betrayed Jesus with a kiss, saying, "the one I will kiss is the man; arrest him" (Matthew 26:48).

Peter denied Jesus three times (Matthew 26:69-75).

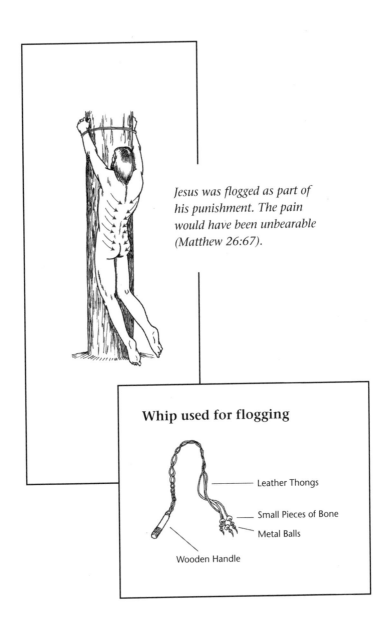

Jesus was flogged as part of his punishment. The pain would have been unbearable (Matthew 26:67).

Whip used for flogging

Leather Thongs

Small Pieces of Bone

Metal Balls

Wooden Handle

After being flogged, carrying the patibulum was
nearly impossible for Jesus.

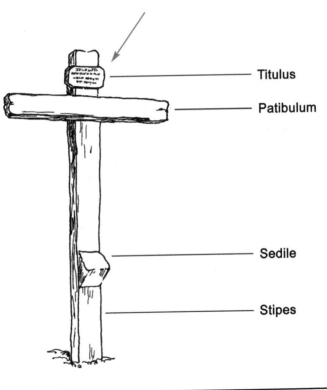

Crucifixion was so common in Jesus' time that the Romans had special names for the parts of the cross.

The charge against Jesus read, "The king of the Jews."

— **Titulus**

— **Patibulum**

— **Sedile**

— **Stipes**

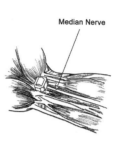

Median Nerve

Typical crucifixion involved being nailed to the cross through the wrists—an excruciatingly painful and humiliating punishment.

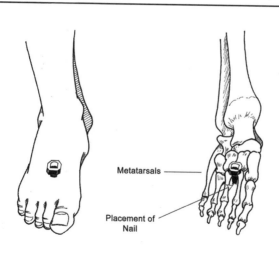

Metatarsals

Placement of Nail

During a crucifixion, a single nail usually was used to pin both feet together to the cross.

Eventually, the victim would be unable to lift himself to take a breath, and he would suffocate.

While the Romans broke the legs of the men who were crucified next to Jesus, they found that Jesus had already died. To make sure, they pierced his side with a spear, probably to puncture his heart (John 19:34).

Joseph of Arimathea and several women took Jesus down and carried him to the tomb (Matthew 27:57-61).

The miracle of resurrection took place three days later, when Jesus rose from the dead.

LUTHER'S SMALL CATECHISM

**A contemporary translation
by Timothy J. Wengert**

Martin Luther had many questions about the Christian faith, and he knew that everyone else did too. For almost 500 years, Luther's Small Catechism has served as a handbook to help people think about the core teachings and practices in the church.

In addition to large questions about the nature of God, Luther offers his thoughts on some details of faith that might be on your mind as well, such as:

- In the Ten Commandments, what exactly does *coveting* mean?

- Does asking for "daily bread" cover all the other food groups too?

- Do you still have to confess your sins if you don't remember doing anything wrong?

THE TEN COMMANDMENTS

You shall have no other gods.

> I the Lord your God am a jealous God,
> punishing children for the iniquity of parents,
> to the third and the fourth generation of those
> who reject me, but showing steadfast love
> to the thousandth generation of those who
> love me and keep my commandments.

You shall not make wrongful use
> of the name of the Lord your God.

Remember the sabbath day, and keep it holy.

Honor your father and your mother.

You shall not murder.

You shall not commit adultery.

You shall not steal.

You shall not bear false witness against
> your neighbor.

You shall not covet your neighbor's house.

You shall not covet your neighbor's wife,
> or male or female slave, or ox, or donkey,
> or anything that belongs to your neighbor.

The First Commandment

You shall have no other gods.

What is this?

Answer: We are to fear, love, and trust God above all things.

- *Bible reading:* Exodus 32

The Second Commandment

You shall not make wrongful use
of the name of the Lord your God.

What is this?

Answer: We are to fear and love God, so that we do not curse, swear, practice magic, lie, or deceive using God's name, but instead use that very name in every time of need to call on, pray to, praise, and give thanks to God.

- *Bible reading:* Leviticus 24:10-16

The Third Commandment

Remember the sabbath day, and keep it holy.

What is this?

Answer: We are to fear and love God, so that we do not despise God's Word or preaching, but instead keep that Word holy and gladly hear and learn it.

- *Bible reading:* Luke 10:38-42

The Fourth Commandment

Honor your father and your mother.

What is this?

Answer: We are to fear and love God, so that we neither despise nor anger our parents and others in authority, but instead honor, serve, obey, love, and respect them.

- *Bible reading:* Luke 2:41-52

The Fifth Commandment

You shall not murder.

What is this?

Answer: We are to fear and love God, so that we neither endanger nor harm the lives of our neighbors, but instead help and support them in all of life's needs.

- *Bible reading:* Genesis 4:1-16

The Sixth Commandment

You shall not commit adultery.

What is this?

Answer: We are to fear and love God, so that we lead pure and decent lives in word and deed, and each of us loves and honors his or her spouse.

- *Bible reading:* 2 Samuel 11

The Seventh Commandment

You shall not steal.

What is this?

Answer: We are to fear and love God, so that we neither take our neighbors' money or property nor cheat them by using shoddy merchandise or crooked deals to obtain it for ourselves, but instead help them to improve and protect their property and income.

- *Bible reading:* Joshua 7:1

The Eighth Commandment

You shall not bear false witness against your neighbor.

What is this?

Answer: We are to fear and love God, so that we do not tell lies about our neighbors, betray or slander them, or destroy their reputations. Instead we are to come to their defense, speak well of them, and interpret everything they do in the best possible light.

- *Bible reading:* Luke 22:54-62

The Ninth Commandment

You shall not covet your neighbor's house.

What is this?

Answer: We are to fear and love God, so that we do not try to trick our neighbors out of their inheritance or property or try to get it for ourselves by claiming to have a legal right to it and the like, but instead be of help and service to them in keeping what is theirs.

The Tenth Commandment

You shall not covet your neighbor's wife,
> or male or female slave, or ox, or donkey,
> or anything that belongs to your neighbor.

What is this?

Answer: We are to fear and love God, so that we do not entice, force, or steal away from our neighbors their spouses, workers, or livestock, but instead urge them to stay and remain loyal to our neighbors.

What then does God say about all these commandments?

Answer: God says the following: "I the Lord your God am a jealous God, punishing children for the iniquity of parents, to the third and the fourth generation of those who reject me, but showing steadfast love to the thousandth generation of those who love me and keep my commandments."

What is this?

Answer: God threatens to punish all who break these commandments. Therefore we are to fear his wrath and not disobey these commandments. However, God promises grace and every good thing to all those who keep these commandments. Therefore we are to love and trust him and gladly act according to his commands.

THE APOSTLES' CREED

I believe in God, the Father almighty,
    creator of heaven and earth.
I believe in Jesus Christ, his only Son, our Lord.
    He was conceived by the power of the Holy Spirit
        and born of the virgin Mary.
    He suffered under Pontius Pilate,
        was crucified, died, and was buried.
    He descended into hell.
    On the third day he rose again.
    He ascended into heaven,
        and is seated at the right hand of the Father.
    He will come again to judge the living and the dead.
I believe in the Holy Spirit,
    the holy catholic Church,
    the communion of saints,
    the forgiveness of sins,
    the resurrection of the body,
    and the life everlasting. Amen.

The First Article: On Creation

I believe in God, the Father almighty,
    creator of heaven and earth.

What is this?

Answer: I believe that God has created me together
with all creatures. God has given me and still preserves
my body and soul: eyes, ears, and all limbs and senses;
reason and all mental faculties. In addition, God daily
and abundantly provides shoes and clothing, food and
drink, house and home, spouse and children, fields,
livestock, and all property—along with all the necessities
and nourishment for this body and life. God protects me
against all danger and shields and preserves me from all
evil. God does all this out of pure, fatherly, and divine
goodness and mercy, without any merit or worthiness of
mine at all! For all of this I owe it to God to thank and
praise, serve and obey him. This is most certainly true.

- *Bible reading:* Psalm 8

The Second Article: On Redemption

I believe in Jesus Christ, his only Son, our Lord.
>He was conceived by the power of the Holy Spirit
>>and born of the virgin Mary.
>He suffered under Pontius Pilate,
>>was crucified, died, and was buried.
>He descended into hell.
>On the third day he rose again.
>He ascended into heaven,
>>and is seated at the right hand of the Father.
>He will come again to judge the living and the dead.

What is this?

Answer: I believe that Jesus Christ, true God, begotten of the Father in eternity, and also true human being, born of the virgin Mary, is my Lord. He has redeemed me, a lost and condemned person. He has purchased and freed me from all sins, from death, and from the power of the devil, not with gold or silver but with his holy, precious blood and with his innocent suffering and death. He has done all this in order that I may belong to him, live under him in his kingdom, and serve him in eternal righteousness, innocence, and blessedness, just as he is risen from the dead and lives and rules in eternity. This is most certainly true.

- ***Bible reading:*** Luke 23:39-46

The Third Article: On Being Made Holy

I believe in the Holy Spirit,
> the holy catholic Church,
> the communion of saints,
> the forgiveness of sins,
> the resurrection of the body,
> and the life everlasting. Amen.

What is this?

Answer: I believe that by my own understanding or strength I cannot believe in Jesus Christ my Lord or come to him, but instead the Holy Spirit has called me through the gospel, enlightened me with his gifts, made me holy, and kept me in the true faith, just as he calls, gathers, enlightens, and makes holy the whole Christian church on earth and keeps it with Jesus Christ in the one common, true faith. Daily in this Christian church the Holy Spirit abundantly forgives all sins—mine and those of all believers. On the last day the Holy Spirit will raise me and all the dead and will give to me and all believers in Christ eternal life. This is most certainly true.

- *Bible reading:* Acts 2

THE LORD'S PRAYER

Our Father, who art in heaven,
hallowed be thy name,
thy kingdom come,
thy will be done,
on earth as it is in heaven.
Give us this day our daily bread;
and forgive us our trespasses,
as we forgive those
who trespass against us;
and lead us not into temptation,
but deliver us from evil.
For thine is the kingdom,
and the power, and the glory,
forever and ever. Amen.

Our Father in heaven,
hallowed be your name,
your kingdom come,
your will be done,
on earth as in heaven.
Give us today our daily bread.
Forgive us our sins
as we forgive those
who sin against us.
Save us from the time of trial
and deliver us from evil.
For the kingdom, the power,
and the glory are yours,
now and forever, Amen.

• *Bible reading:* Mark 14:32-42

Introduction

Our Father in heaven.

What is this?

Answer: With these words God wants to attract us, so that we believe he is truly our Father and we are truly his children, in order that we may ask him boldly and with complete confidence, just as loving children ask their loving father.*

The First Petition**

Hallowed be your name.

What is this?

Answer: It is true that God's name is holy in itself, but we ask in this prayer that it may also become holy in and among us.

How does this come about?

Answer: Whenever the Word of God is taught clearly and purely and we, as God's children, also live holy lives according to it. To this end help us, dear Father in heaven! However, whoever teaches and lives otherwise than the Word of God teaches, dishonors God's name among us. Preserve us from this, heavenly Father!

- **Bible reading:** Acts 13:13-47

---

* Luther added this explanation to the Small Catechism in 1531, when his oldest child was five years old.

** The word *petition* means "request."

The Second Petition

Your kingdom come.

What is this?

Answer: In fact, God's kingdom comes on its own without our prayer, but we ask in this prayer that it may also come to us.

How does this come about?

Answer: Whenever our heavenly Father gives us his Holy Spirit, so that through the Holy Spirit's grace we believe God's Holy Word and live godly lives here in time and hereafter in eternity.

• *Bible reading:* Luke 15:8-10

The Third Petition

Your will be done,
on earth as in heaven.

What is this?

Answer: In fact, God's good and gracious will comes about without our prayer, but we ask in this prayer that it may also come about in and among us.

How does this come about?

Answer: Whenever God breaks and hinders every evil scheme and will of the devil, the world, and our flesh that would not allow us to hallow God's name and would prevent the coming of his kingdom. And God's will comes about whenever God strengthens us and keeps us steadfast in his Word and in faith until the end of our lives. This is God's gracious and good will.

- *Bible reading:* Matthew 27:27-31

The Fourth Petition

Give us today our daily bread.

What is this?

Answer: In fact, God gives daily bread without our prayer, even to all evil people, but we ask in this prayer that God cause us to recognize what our daily bread is and to receive it with thanksgiving.

What then does "daily bread" mean?

Answer: Everything our bodies need such as food, drink, clothing, shoes, house, home, fields, livestock, money, property, an upright spouse, upright children, upright workers, upright and faithful rulers, good government, good weather, peace, health, decency, honor, good friends, faithful neighbors, and the like.

- *Bible reading:* John 6:8-10

The Fifth Petition

Forgive us our sins
    as we forgive those
        who sin against us.

What is this?

Answer: We ask in this prayer that our heavenly Father would not regard our sins or deny these petitions on their account, for we are worthy of nothing for which we ask, nor have we earned it. Instead we ask that God would give us all things by grace, for we sin daily and indeed earn only punishment. So, on the other hand, we, too, truly want to forgive heartily and do good gladly to those who sin against us.

- *Bible reading:* Matthew 18:23-35

The Sixth Petition

Save us from the time of trial.*

What is this?

Answer: It is true that God tempts no one, but we ask in this prayer that God would preserve and keep us, so that the devil, the world, and our flesh may not deceive us or mislead us into false belief, despair, and other great and shameful sins, and that, although we may be attacked by them, we may finally prevail and gain the victory.

• *Bible reading:* Matthew 4:4-11

The Seventh Petition

And deliver us from evil.

What is this?

Answer: We ask in this prayer, as in a summary, that our Father in heaven may deliver us from all kinds of evil—affecting body or soul, property or reputation—and at last, when our final hour comes, may grant us a blessed end and take us by grace from this valley of tears to himself in heaven.

• *Bible reading:* Matthew 15:21-28

---

* The version of the Lord's Prayer used by Luther employed the word *temptation* in place of "the time of trial."

Conclusion*

For the kingdom, the power,
and the glory are yours,
now and forever. Amen.

What is this?

Answer: That I should be certain that such petitions are acceptable to and heard by our Father in heaven, for God himself commanded us to pray like this and has promised to hear us. "Amen, amen" means "Yes, yes, it is going to come about just like this."

---

* Some later editions of the catechism, printed after Luther's death, add this conclusion, commonly called the Doxology. Although found in Erasmus's editions of the Greek New Testament and in Luther's translation of that into German, Luther himself consistently followed the medieval practice and omitted it.

THE SACRAMENT OF HOLY BAPTISM

❶ What is Baptism?

Answer: Baptism is not simply plain water. Instead it is water used according to God's command and connected with God's Word.

What then is this Word of God?

Answer: Where our Lord Jesus Christ says in Matthew 28:19, "Go therefore and make disciples of all nations, baptizing them in the name of the Father and of the Son and of the Holy Spirit."

❷ What gifts or benefits does Baptism grant?

Answer: It brings about forgiveness of sins, redeems from death and the devil, and gives eternal salvation to all who believe it, as the Word and promise of God declare.

What is this Word and promise of God?

Answer: Where our Lord Jesus Christ says in Mark 16:16, "The one who believes and is baptized will be saved; but the one who does not believe will be condemned."

For more information, see "The Anatomy of a Baptism" on page 34.

❸ How can water do such great things?

Answer: Clearly the water does not do it, but the Word of God, which is with, in, and among the water, and faith, which trusts this Word of God in the water. For without the Word of God the water is plain water and not a baptism, but with the Word of God it is a baptism, that is, a grace-filled water of life and a "bath of the new birth in the Holy Spirit." As St. Paul says to Titus in 3:5-8, "He saved us, not because of any works of righteousness that we had done, but according to his mercy, through the water of rebirth and renewal by the Holy Spirit. This Spirit he poured out on us richly through Jesus Christ our Savior, so that, having been justified by his grace, we might become heirs according to the hope of eternal life. The saying is sure." *

---

* In Luther's translation of Titus, the last line reads, "This is most certainly true," as in the explanation to the Apostles' Creed and the meaning of *Amen* in the Lord's Prayer.

❹ What then is the significance of such a baptism with water?

Answer: It signifies that the old person in us with all sins and evil desires is to be drowned through daily sorrow for sin and repentance, and that daily a new person is to come forth and rise up to live before God in righteousness and purity forever.

Where is this written?

Answer: St. Paul says in Romans 6:3-4, "Do you not know that all of us who have been baptized into Christ Jesus were baptized into his death? Therefore we have been buried with him by baptism into death, so that, just as Christ was raised from the dead by the glory of the Father, so we too might walk in newness of life."

* *Bible reading:* Matthew 28:16-20

CONFESSION

What is confession?

Answer: Confession consists of two parts. One is that we confess our sins. The other is that we receive the absolution, that is, forgiveness, from the pastor as from God himself and by no means doubt but firmly believe that our sins are thereby forgiven before God in heaven.

Which sins is a person to confess?

Before God one is to acknowledge the guilt for all sins, even those of which we are not aware, as we do in the Lord's Prayer. However, before the pastor we are to confess only those sins of which we are aware and which trouble us.

Which sins are these?

Here reflect on your place in life in light of the Ten Commandments: whether you are father, mother, son, daughter, employer, employee; whether you have been disobedient, unfaithful, lazy; whether you have harmed anyone by word or deed; whether you have stolen, neglected, wasted, or injured anything.

For more information, see "How to Confess Your Sins and Receive Forgiveness" on page 103.

Individual Confession and Forgiveness*

The confession made by the penitent is protected from disclosure. The pastor is obligated to respect at all times the confidential nature of a confession. The pastor greets the penitent. When the penitent has knelt, the pastor begins:

Pastor: Are you prepared to make your confession?

Response: I am.

The pastor and penitent say the psalm together.

O Lord, open my lips, and my mouth shall
    declare your praise.
Had you desired it, I would have offered sacrifice,
    but you take no delight in burnt offerings.
The sacrifice of God is a troubled spirit;
    a broken and contrite heart, O God,
    you will not despise.
Have mercy on me, O God,
    according to your lovingkindness;
    in your great compassion blot out my offenses.
Wash me through and through from my wickedness,
    and cleanse me from my sin.
PSALM 51:16-18, 1-2

Pastor: You have come to make confession before God. In Christ you are free to confess before me, a pastor in his Church, the sins of which you are aware and the sins which trouble you.

---

*   This service of individual confession from *Lutheran Book of Worship* replaces the form used in Luther's day.

Response: I confess before God that I am guilty of many sins. Especially I confess before you that ... *

*The penitent confesses those sins which are known and those which disturb or grieve him/her.***

For all this I am sorry and I pray for forgiveness. I want to do better.

---

* An early version of Luther's Small Catechism prepared especially for school children suggests a student might say, "As a student I have not performed my duties diligently. For I have not always done the daily work my teachers have assigned, but have often angered and offended them with my negligence, so that they have had to reprimand me because I have not cared about my studies. I also confess that I have spoken and acted indecently, have often become angry with my peers, have often complained about my teachers, and the like."

** At this point Luther reminds us: "If some individuals do not find themselves burdened by these or greater sins, they are not to worry, nor are they to search for or invent further sins and thereby turn confession into torture. Instead mention one or two that you are aware of and let that be enough. If you are aware of no sins at all (which is really quite unlikely), then do not mention any in particular, but instead receive forgiveness on the basis of the general confession that you made to God in the pastor's presence."

The pastor may then engage the penitent in pastoral conversation, offering admonition and comfort from the Holy Scriptures. Then they say together:

Have mercy on me, O God,
>according to your lovingkindness;
>in your great compassion blot out my offenses.

Create in me a clean heart, O God,
>and renew a right spirit within me.

Cast me not away from your presence,
>and take not your Holy Spirit from me.

Restore to me the joy of your salvation,
>and uphold me with your free Spirit.

PSALM: 51:1, 11-13

The pastor stands and faces the penitent or remains seated and turns toward the penitent.

Pastor: Do you believe that the word of forgiveness I speak to you comes from God himself?

Response: Yes, I believe.

The pastor lays both hands on the head of the penitent.

Pastor: God is merciful and blesses you. By the command of our Lord Jesus Christ, I, a called and ordained servant of the Word, forgive you your sins in the name of the Father, and of the Son, and of the Holy Spirit.

Response: Amen.

The penitent may pray silently in thanksgiving, or may pray together with the pastor. *

The Lord is full of compassion and mercy,
    slow to anger and of great kindness.
He will not always accuse us,
    nor will he keep his anger forever.
He has not dealt with us according to our sins,
    nor rewarded us according to our wickedness.
For as the heavens are high above the earth,
    so is his mercy great upon those who fear him.
As far as the east is from the west,
    so far has he removed our sins from us.
As a father cares for his children,
    so does the Lord care for those who fear him.

PSALM 103:8-13

Glory to the Father, and to the Son, and to the Holy Spirit; as it was in the beginning, is now, and will be forever. Amen.

Pastor: Blessed are those whose sins have been forgiven, whose evil deeds have been forgotten. Rejoice in the Lord, and go in peace.

---

*   Luther adds, "A pastor, by using additional passages of Scripture, will in fact be able to comfort and encourage to faith those whose consciences are heavily burdened or who are distressed and under attack."

THE SACRAMENT OF HOLY COMMUNION

❶ What is the Sacrament of the Altar?

Answer: It is the true body and blood of our Lord Jesus Christ under the bread and wine, instituted by Christ himself for us Christians to eat and to drink.

Where is this written?

Answer: The holy evangelists, Matthew, Mark and Luke, and St. Paul write thus:

In the night
 in which he was betrayed,
 our Lord Jesus took bread,
 and gave thanks; broke it,
 and gave it to his disciples,
 saying: Take and eat;
 this is my body, given for you.
Do this for the remembrance of me.
 Again, after supper,
 he took the cup, gave thanks,
 and gave it for all to drink,
 saying: This cup is
 the new covenant* in my blood,
 shed for you and for all people
 for the forgiveness of sin.
Do this for the remembrance of me.

---

*   *Covenant* means "promise."

❷ What is the benefit of such eating and drinking?

Answer: The words "given for you" and "shed for you ... for the forgiveness of sin" show us that forgiveness of sin, life, and salvation are given to us in the sacrament through these words, because where there is forgiveness of sin, there is also life and salvation.

❸ How can bodily eating and drinking do such a great thing?

Answer: Eating and drinking certainly do not do it, but rather the words that are recorded: "given for you" and "shed for you ... for the forgiveness of sin." These words, when accompanied by the physical eating and drinking, are the essential thing in the sacrament, and whoever believes in these very words has what they declare and state, namely, "forgiveness of sin."

❹ Who, then, receives this sacrament worthily?

Answer: Fasting and bodily preparation are in fact a fine external discipline, but a person who has faith in these words, "given for you" and "shed for you ... for the forgiveness of sin," is really worthy and well prepared. However, a person who does not believe these words or doubts them is unworthy and unprepared, because the words "for you" require truly believing hearts.

- *Bible reading:* Matthew 26:26-28

For more information, see
"How to Receive Communion"
on page 36.

MORNING AND EVENING PRAYER

How the head of the house is to teach the members of the household to say morning and evening blessings.

The Morning Blessing

In the morning, as soon as you get out of bed, you are to make the sign of the holy cross and say:

> Under the care of God the Father, Son, and Holy Spirit. Amen.

Then, kneeling or standing, say the Apostles' Creed and the Lord's Prayer. If you wish, you may recite this little prayer as well:

> I give thanks to you, my heavenly Father, through Jesus Christ your dear Son, that you have protected me through the night from all harm and danger and I ask that you would also protect me today from sin and every danger, so that my life and actions may please you. Into your hands I commend myself: my body, my soul, and all that is mine. Let your holy angel be with me, so that the wicked foe may have no power over me. Amen.

After singing a hymn, or whatever else may serve your devotion, you are to go to your work joyfully.

The Evening Blessing

In the evening, when you go to bed, you are to make the sign of the holy cross and say:

> Under the care of God the Father, Son, and Holy Spirit. Amen.

Then, kneeling or standing, say the Apostles' Creed and the Lord's Prayer. If you wish, you may recite this little prayer as well:

> I give thanks to you, my heavenly Father, through Jesus Christ your dear Son, that you have graciously protected me today, and I ask you to forgive me all my sins, where I have done wrong, and graciously to protect me tonight. For into your hands I commend myself: my body, my soul, and all that is mine. Let your holy angel be with me, so that the wicked foe may have no power over me. Amen.

Then you are to go to sleep quickly and cheerfully.

- *Bible reading:* Psalm 78:1-8

For more information about morning devotions and evening prayers, see "Three Essential Personal Spiritual Rituals" on page 98.

BLESSINGS AT MEALS

How the head of the house is to teach members of the household to offer blessing and thanksgiving at meals.

The Table Blessing

The children and the members of the household are to come devoutly to the table, fold their hands, and recite:

> The eyes of all look to you, and you give them their food in due season. You open your hand, satisfying the desire of every living thing.*
>
>   PSALM 145:15-16

Then they are to recite the Lord's Prayer and the following prayer:

> Lord God, heavenly Father, bless us and these your gifts, which we receive from your bountiful goodness through Jesus Christ our Lord. Amen.

---

* Luther translates this last line, "satisfies every living thing with delight," and adds that "delight" means that all animals receive enough to eat to make them joyful and of good cheer, because human worry and greed prevent such delight.

Thanksgiving

Similarly, after eating they should in the same manner fold their hands and recite devoutly:

Praise the Lord! O give thanks to the Lord, for he is good, for his steadfast love endures forever. He gives to the animals their food, and to the young ravens when they cry. His delight is not in the strength of the horse, nor his pleasure in the speed of a runner; but the Lord takes pleasure in those who fear him, in those who hope in his steadfast love.

PSALM 106:1; 136:1, 26; 147:9-11

Then recite the Lord's Prayer and the following prayer:

We give thanks to you, Lord God our Father, through Jesus Christ our Lord for all your benefits, you who live and reign forever. Amen.

- *Bible reading:* Psalm 65:9-13

For more information about saying mealtime grace, see "Three Essential Personal Spiritual Rituals" on page 98.

NOTES & STUFF

NOTES & STUFF

NOTES & STUFF

NOTES & STUFF

NOTES & STUFF

NOTES & STUFF

NOTES & STUFF

NOTES & STUFF

NOTES & STUFF

NOTES & STUFF

NOTES & STUFF

NOTES & STUFF

NOTES & STUFF